Bibliography of Australian Education

from colonial times to 1972

compiled by Cecily Brown

Bibliography of Australian Education

Bibliography of Australian Education

from colonial times to 1972

compiled by

Cecily Brown

 AUSTRALIAN COUNCIL FOR EDUCATIONAL RESEARCH

Published by Australian Council for Educational Research
Frederick Street, Hawthorn, Victoria 3122
Copyright © ACER 1973
Printed by Brown Prior Anderson Pty Ltd

National Library of Australia Card No.
and ISBN 0 85563 093 0
Dewey Decimal Classification No. 016.370994
Registered in Australia for transmission
by post as a book

Contents

Introduction

Preparation of this bibliography was inspired by Herbert Roth's 'A bibliography of New Zealand education' (NZCER, 1964). Work was begun on an Australian bibliography by Mr R. V. McSweeney when he was a member of Department of External Studies, University of Queensland, but he was forced to abandon the bibliography because of pressure of other work.

A new start was made late in 1970 at ACER and it soon became apparent that a comprehensive edition would require several years of patient hunting and listing. It was decided to publish this edition using entries collected to the end of 1972 and to give the bibliography a wide circulation as soon as possible. Users will find that this first edition is therefore incomplete. Work has already begun on a revised and expanded edition which will include works published up to 1975, and it is hoped that this second edition will be ready for publication in 1976. Current annual bibliographies are being published in each annual volume of the 'Australian education index' and these supplement this publication. Sources consulted in the compilation of the bibliography are listed on page 171.

The printed catalogue of the Mitchell Library has been of very great assistance in checking items. Many of the titles listed have been seen at the ACER library, the State Library of Victoria and its specialized Australian collection in the La Trobe Library, the National Library of Australia, and the Library of New South Wales and the Mitchell Library, Sydney.

Users of this bibliography will find errors and omissions. They are asked to send notice of these to the compiler, Mrs Cecily Brown, the Australian Council for Educational Research, PO Box 210, Hawthorn, Victoria 3122, so that corrections and additions can be made and incorporated in the revised edition.

SELECTION OF ENTRIES

Entries are included for works published up to and including 1972. Australian education has been given a wide interpretation to include works published by Australians, in Australia or about Australian education. Duplicated and roneoed material has been included as well as printed material because its exclusion would frequently mean that important works would be omitted.

Journals and journal articles, calendars, courses of study, guides, handbooks, textbooks, legislation, government reports, and theses have been omitted. It may be desirable to include some of this material in a later edition of this bibliography. Comments are invited from users.

ARRANGEMENT

This bibliography has been arranged by broad subject headings, with works arranged chronologically within subjects. This gives only a general approach to subjects; to find entries for a specific subject, and to find all works on a subject, the subject index should be used.

In a few cases where a single work is of importance to more than one subject area, it has been included in each relevant section. References are made in the text to related subjects. Wherever possible entries have been included in the subject and name indexes for essays within collections of material. The compiler had hoped to see all the material before including it, but this has not been possible. Subject allocation has therefore been hazardous at times, depending on other opinions. Corrections of disputed subject allocations would be appreciated.

For those who are looking for material by particular authors, a name index is provided. It includes authors, joint authors, biographers, and names of institutions, associations, conferences, series, etc. A detailed series index will be included in the next edition.

FORM OF ENTRIES

Full details about author, title, and publisher are given. If place and publisher have been omitted, this is because they are the same as the body already mentioned in the entry. When the work does not bear date or publisher, and an estimation has been made, this is indicated by square brackets, e.g. [1962?], [the Author?]. Notes have been included in some cases where a further explanation was considered necessary.

A   19th Century Views of Australian Education

1 Publications 1831 to 1899

This section includes works published between 1831 and 1899 and
reflects educational theories and policies of the time. Important and
recurrent themes are the debates on the type of educational system
best suited to the developing Australian states, and on the 'national'
system which was to provide free, secular schools. Entries for this
section are included in the name and subject indexes.

1831 (1) LANG, J.D. Account of the steps taken in England with a view
to the establishment of an academical institution or college in
New South Wales. Syd, Stephens & Stokes, 1831. 28p.

1834 (2) MURRAY, H.N. The schoolmaster in Van Dieman's Land: a
practical treatise on education for the use of parents and others
not professed teachers. Hobart Town, A. Bent, 1934. 97p.

1835 (3) SOUTH Australian School Society. A plan for the establishment
of schools in the new colony of South Australia. Plymouth,
England, W.C. Cox, [1835?]. 4p.
Also published about 1835 by Maddox (Printer), Dockhead,
Bermondsey, England.

1836 (4) GENERAL education: resolutions at a meeting of Protestants,
representing the Episcopalian, the Presbyterian, the Independent,
the Baptist and the Wesleyan denominations of Christians in New
South Wales. Syd, H. Bull, 1836. 6p.

(5) THERRY, R. Explanation of the plan of the Irish National
Schools, showing its peculiar adaptation to New South Wales. Syd,
A. Cohen, 1836. 14p.

1839 (6) AUSTRALIAN School Society. A concise statement of the
principle of the British and Foreign School Society; with a sketch
of the Society's history, and systems of teaching. Syd, J. Tegg,
1839. 60p.

(7) BROUGHTON, W.G. The speech of the Lord Bishop of
Australia, in the Legislative Council, upon the resolutions for
establishing a system of general education. Syd, J. Tegg, 1839.
44p.

(8) HUTCHINS, W. A letter on the school question. Hobart Town,
W.G. Elliston, 1839. 16p.

1840 (9) BERWICK, J. and Turner, T. A letter to parents on the education of their children. Lond, Clowes, 1840. 12p.
A moral essay on the education and upbringing of children.

(10) BURTON, W. W. The state of religion and education in New South Wales. Lond, J. Cross, 1840. 470p.

1843 (11) LOCH, J. D. An account of the introduction and effects of the system of general religious education established in Van Dieman's Land in 1839. Hobart Town, J. C. Macdougall, 1843. 172p.

1846 (12) CHRISTS College, Tasmania. Hobart Town, W. G. Elliston, 1846. 28p.
Sets out the steps taken by the Bishop of Tasmania for the found-ation of the College, and a general history of other scholastic institutions in Tasmania.

1848 (13) BOYD, H. V. Letters on education; addressed to a friend in the bush. Syd, W. & F. Ford, 1848. 168p.
'An attempt to assist bush mothers in the education of their children, other means of instruction being absent. One of the earliest Australian educational treatises'.

(14) CATHOLICUS. An original essay on popular education, its general merits, and special adaptation to the circumstances of the Colony of New South Wales. Syd, W. G. Moore, 1848. 16p.

1850 (15) DUNCAN, W. A. Lecture on national education, delivered at the School of Arts, Brisbane on 20 June, 1850. Brisb, J. Swan, 1850. 24p.
The first booklet printed in Queensland.

(16) GREGSON, T. G. Speech ... in the Legislative Council on the state of public education in Van Dieman's Land. Hobart Town, J. C. Macdougall, 1850. 32p.

(17) WALLACE, J. Lecture on the denominational system of education. Syd, Kemp & Fairfax, [1850?]. 16p.

(18) WOOLLS, W. Lines written to commemorate the passing of a bill to incorporate and endow a university to be called the University of Sydney. Parramatta, NSW, E. Mason, 1850. 8p.

1851 (19) PAPERS relating to the University of Sydney, and to the University College, Sydney, New South Wales. Lond, R. Taylor, 1851. 36p.

1853 (20) CAMPBELL, C. Remarks on national education with reference to the Colony of Victoria. Melb, B. Lucas, 1853. 4p.

(21) RUSDEN, G. W. National education. Melb, Argus Office, 1853. 380p.
Chapter 10 by H. C. E. Childers deals with New South Wales, Tasmania, South Australia and Victoria.

1854 (22) MACGOWAN, J. The science of instruction; or The laws of nature on the subject of teaching. Adel, Hussey & Shawyer, 1854. 12p.

1855 (23) NEMO, pseud. Sir William Denison and education. Syd, J. Cook, 1855. 8p.

1856 (24) DAVITT, A. Origin and progress of the national system of education; its real principles, and special adaptability to the circumstances of a mixed community. Melb, Wilson, Mackinnon & Fairfax, 1856. 28p.

(25) EDUCATION; thoughts [in verse] on the mental condition to which it is applicable. Melb, Wilson, Mackinnon & Fairfax, 1856. 36p.

(26) HEARN, W. H. A lecture on the proposed formation of adult educational classes. Melb, Wilson, Mackinnon & Fairfax, 1856. 8p.

(27) MACARTNEY, H. B. State aid to religion and education. Melb, J. N. Sayers, 1856. 32p.
Very Rev H. B. Macartney, DD, was Dean of Melbourne at the time of writing.

(28) WESLEYAN Committee of Education. A statement and correspondence with the government relative to Wesleyan day schools in Victoria. Melb, 1856. 20p.

1857 (29) HOLT, T. Two speeches on the subject of education in New South Wales. Syd, D.L. Welch, 1857. 44p.

(30) NATIONAL education; a series of letters in defence of the national system, against the attacks of an anonymous writer in the Sydney Morning Herald, by the teachers of the National Schools of Sydney. Syd, Empire General Steam Printing Office, 1857. 48p.

(31) A PLEA for common schools; by a colonist. Syd, Reading & Wellbank, 1857. 16p.

(32) SYMONS, J. C. What is the best system of education for Victoria? An essay. Melb, G. Nichols, 1857. 22p.

1858 (33) DARLING, J. Education; a sermon. Melb, Lucas Bros, 1858. 12p.

(34) McINTYRE, W. The Presbyterian College question; being the substance of two speeches delivered in the Synod of Eastern Australia, in November 1857. Syd, J.L. Sherriff, 1858. 60p.

(35) NEW South Wales. Board of National Education. Statement explanatory of the system of education administered by the National Board of New South Wales. Syd, G. Taylor, 1858. 24p.
Second edition published in 1861.

1859 (36) COCKBURN, H. M. General education considered with reference to the antagonistic bearings on it of the principles of the national system defined as socialism, socinianism, and infidelity: a lecture. Syd, J. L. Sherriff, 1859. 26p.

(37) A LECTURE on state aid to religion, to ecclesiastical colleges, and to denominational schools, by a student of theology. Wollongong, T. Garnett, 1859. 20p.

1860 (38) MACARTNEY, H. B. Education in Victoria for the future; a lecture. Melb, S. Mullen, 1860. 20p.

(39) MACDONALD, D. Denominational education in Victoria; a lecture. Melb, R & M, 1860. 10p.

(40) MORISON, A. Education in other lands; a review of popular education among the principal nations of the earth. Melb, M. K. Armstrong, [1860?]. 24p.

1862 (41) DENISON, Sir W. T. Systems of education: a lecture. Madras, Military Male Orphan Asylum Press, 1862. 52p.

(42) HIGINBOTHAM, G. Self education: a lecture. Melb, Blundell & Ford, 1862. 24p.

1865 (43) MOORE, J. S. University reform, its urgency and reasonableness; an oration. Syd, H. Cole, [1865?]. 24p.

(44) WILKINS, W. National education; an exposition of the national system of New South Wales. Syd, A. W. Douglas, 1865. 58p.

1866 (45) MUECKE, C. National schools for South Australia. Adel, Platts, 1866. 20p.

(46) PARKES, Sir H. Public education; speech ... September 12 1866. Syd, Sherriff Downing, 1866. 38p.

(47) PUBLIC instruction: a letter to the Hon. Henry Parkes, MP, Colonial Secretary of New South Wales, by a Colonist. Syd, Gibbs, Shallard, 1866. 8p.

1867 (48) COOPER, J. Education, viewed in some of its higher aspects. Melb, G. Robertson, 1867. 16p.

(49) HIGINBOTHAM, G. Public instruction: speeches. Melb, S. Mullen, 1867. 24p.

(50) ROBERTSON, A. The past and future of the education question. Melb, Age Office, 1867. 16p.

(51) SKINNER, S. Educational essays; or, Practical observations on the intellectual and moral training and scholastic discipline of youth; with inquiries and remarks illustrating the respective advantages of home and colonial education; and suggesting methods by which the necessity of leaving the colony in order to obtain a liberal education may be superseded. Melb, G. Robertson, 1867. 148p.

1868 (52) ROBERTSON, A. Letter to Hon James M'Culloch on the educational question with a special view to the solution of the Roman Catholic difficulty. Melb, Mason, Firth & Co, 1868. 12p.

1869 (53) A. , C. S. Education and the rights of women. Adel, Gall, 1868. 12p.

(54) BROWNE, F. H. A discourse on education, suggested by the laying of the foundation-stone of the Public School, Windsor. Windsor, NSW, Benjamin Isaacs, 1869. 24p.

(55) NAYLER, B. S. Education, secular and religious instruction; a lecture. Melb, Evans Bros, 1869. 19p.

1870 (56) PARKES, Sir H. The Public Schools Act. Syd, J. Ferguson, 1870. 26p.

1871 (57) A. , J. B. Young Victoria; a contribution in aid of national education. Melb, Mason, Firth & M'Cutcheon, 1871. 32p.

(58) BROWNLESS, A. C. An address delivered in the University of Melbourne at the annual matriculation of students, on 4 March 1871. Melb, Stillwell & Knight, 1871. 12p.
Includes a history of the University.

(59) EDUCATION: defects of the common school system, and proposed new system, based on district population and entire local management. Melb, Mason, Firth & M'Cutcheon, 1871. 24p.

(60) RUSDEN, H. K. The Bishop of Melbourne's theory of education, Melb, R. Bell, 1871. 8p.
Signed 'Hokor'.

1872 (61) HEARN, W. E. Payment by results in primary education. Melb, G. Robertson, 1872. 22p.

(62) MIRAMS, J. Education; our present system reviewed with suggestions for its alteration and improvement. Melb, the Author, 1872. 16p.

(63) STEPHEN, J. W. Speech on the first reading of the Education - al Bill. Melb, Fergusson & Moore, 1872. 16p.
The bill provided for free, compulsory and secular education in Victoria. J. W. Stephen became the first Minister of Public Instruction in Victoria, 1872-74.

1873 (64) McCULLOCH, C. National education and the claims of the Bible; a lecture. Brisb, A. Cleghorn, 1873. 34p.

1874 (65) BEECHER, H. W. Compulsory education; a lecture. Melb, Mason, Firth & M'Cutcheon, 1874. 24p.
'A plea for universal and thorough culture for the masses'. The lecture was given in New York in 1874.

(66) EDUCATION v. religion. Syd, J. Ferguson, 1874. 48p.

(67) STEPHEN, Sir A. Public school system; address. Syd, Cook, 1874. 12p.

1875 (68) O'MALLEY, J. Secular education and Christian civilization. Melb, T. E. Verga, 1875. 24p.

(69) PARKES, Sir H. Public education; speech on the education question June 18 1815. Syd, Gibbs, Shalland, 1875. 18p.
A defence of the Public Schools Act 1866 which made education undenominational.

(70) A PLEA for free education. Adel, W. K. Thomas, 1875. 12p.

(71) STUART, Sir A. Primary education; speech on the education debate. Syd, J. Cook, 1875. 24p.

(72) WHITE, J. S. Lecture on education; national, secular, compulsory, and free. West Maitland, NSW, H. Thomas, 1875. 20p.

1876 (73) COOK, C. Lectures on education, three in number. Syd, Lee & Ross, 1876. 52p.

(74) MOREHEAD, R. A. A. Primary education as administered in New South Wales; a letter. Syd, R. Bone, 1876. 70p.

(75) REES, R. Technical education; an address. Adel, W. K. Thomas, 1876. 10p.

(76) ROBINSON, Sir H. A speech on culture and education delivered at the University of Sydney, on 24 June 1876 by His Excellency ... the Governor of New South Wales. Syd, G. Robertson, 1876. 8p.

(77) STATE system of education in Victoria; its absolute perfec-. tions and manifold blessings, indicated in its three great and glorious characteristics 'secular, compulsory and free'. A sermon recently preached in Melbourne by an Anglican clergyman and published at the request and expense of some members of his congregation. Melb, Walker, 1876. 12p.
A plea for the Sunday schools of Victoria.

1878 (78) O'SHANNASSY, Sir J. Primary education in Victoria; speeches. Melb, F. F. Balliere, 1878. 72p.

1879 (79) CARTER, F. H. The teacher in class; a paper read ... on Thursday 27 February 1879. Adel, Webb, Vandon & Pritchard, 1879. 4p.
About methods of teaching religion in schools.

(80) ROMAN Catholic Church, Australia. Catholic education: a pastoral letter of the Archbishop and Bishops exercising jurisdiction in New South Wales. Syd, F. Cunninghame, 1879. 20p.

(81) SMITH, Rev Canon and Jefferies, J. T. The Roman Catholic Church and the education question. Brisb, Rowney, 1879. 32p.

1880 (82) ADDRESS on school education. Hobart Town, Mercury Steam Press Office, 1880. 16p.
'Re-printed in the belief that it will be of service to the cause of education in Tasmania' (note on verso of title page).

(83) BADHAM, C. Primary education. Syd, Gibbs, Shallard [1880]. 14p.
His views on the Public Instruction Act of 1880, which withdrew the state grant of financial support to denominational schools in New South Wales.

(84) BEG, W. Letters on public education in New South Wales. Syd, F. White, 1880. 30p.

(85) DIXON, W.A. Technical education; outlines of a practical scheme to carry out a system of technical education through the Schools of Art in New South Wales, based on that now in operation in the Technical College in connection with the Sydney Institution. Syd, Colonial Publishing Society, 1880. 20p.

(86) LYNCH, J.T. Letters on the Education Bill of New South Wales, 1880. Syd, F. Cunninghame, 1880. 54p.
Monsignor Lynch writes on behalf of those 'who will not divorce Education from Religion'.

(87) PARKES, Sir H. Public instruction; speech delivered on the opening of the public school, Blayney, 25 May 1880. Syd, G. Robertson, 1880. 16p.
'Reprinted, with correction, from the special report of the Sydney Morning Herald'.

(88) PLUMMER, J. Technical education; suggestions for a practical scheme intended primarily for the artisan class of New South Wales. Syd, H. Solomon, 1880. 12p.

1882 (89) CANAWAY, A.P. The Tasmanian Scholarship Scheme considered in a letter to the Hon Henry Butler, President of the Council for Education. Hobart, J. Walch, 1882. 12p.

1883 (90) TOMKINSON, S. Education Bill; speeches. Adel, W.K. Thomas, 1883. 8p.

1885 (91) HOARE, B. The true story of the Victorian Education Act, its merits and defects. Geelong, G. Mercer, 1885. 24p.

(92) MICHIE, Sir A. Observations on the working of the Victorian Education Act, and on the alleged Roman Catholic grievance. Melb, G. Robertson, 1885. 56p.

(93) TAYLOR, A.J. Free education: a rejoinder. Hobart, Mercury Office, 1885. 2p.

(94) TAYLOR, A.J. Free education; a word in favour of the system. Hobart, Mercury Office, 1885. 4p.

(95) TAYLOR, A.J. Overpressure in education. Hobart, Mercury Office, 1885. 8p.

1886 (96) BEAN, E. and Sly, J.D. High schools versus scholarships; an enquiry into the merits of the two systems. Bathurst, NSW, Glyndwr Whalan, 1886. 8p.

(97) CONIGRAVE, J. F. Technical education in New South Wales; a paper. Adel, Burden & Bonython, 1886. 20p.

(98) FAIRFIELD, pseud. Criticisms on state education in Victoria ... a selection of letters which appeared in the Ballarat Star. Ballarat, Curtis, 1886. 44p.

(99) MARSHALL, J. Education of the people; the corpse revived, by a young Australian. Melb, Wright, Walter, 1886. 48p.
'A pamphlet on the defects of the Victorian Education Act and their "safe cure" including a cure for the Catholic difficulty' (subtitle).

(100) PEARSON, C. H. The Ontario school system. Melb, S. Mullen, 1886. 24p.
A comparison with the Victorian system, in the latter's favour.

(101) RUSSELL, J. The schools of Great Britain; sketches of the educational systems of the colonies and India. Lond, Collins, 1886. 228p.
Part 2 and an appendix deal with secondary education in Australia and New Zealand.

(102) WILKINS, W. The principles that underlie the art of teaching. Syd, T. Richards, 1886. 72p.

1887 (103) COMBES, E. Education in Australia; a paper. Lond, C. F. Hodgson, 1887. 28p.

1888 (104) BLACKMORE, H. G. On the value of physical education and its practical introduction into schools. Syd, Gibbs, Shallard, 1888. 22p.

1889 (105) PEARSON, C. H. Religious teaching in schools; a speech. Melb, S. Mullen, 1889. 32p.
C. H. Pearson, LL D, was Minister of Public Instruction in Victoria, 1886-90.

1891 (106) GRASBY, W. C. Our public schools; an educational policy for Australia. Adel, Hussey & Gillingham, 1891. 64p.
Appendix has plans for school buildings.

(107) GRASBY, W. C. Teaching in three continents; personal notes on the educational systems of the world. Lond, Cassell, 1891. 360p.
Includes a section on his experience in Australia.

(108) HILL, A. W. Education. Terowie, SA, Enterprise Office, 1891. 4p.

(109) STUART, Sir T. P. A. A review of university life in Australasia with its conditions and surroundings in 1891. Lond, Spottiswoode, 1892. 44p.

(110) WHITFIELD, M. J. The Free Education Bill: a historical
sketch. Adel, Hussey & Gillingham, 1891. 36p.
Objections to the system of free education in South Australia.

1893 (111) HILL, H. Education: the school systems of Australia.
Napier, NZ, Daily Telegraph Office, 1893. 14p.

(112) SUTHERLAND, G. Moral training in our public schools;
a letter to the Minister of Public Instruction in New South Wales.
Syd, Epworth, 1893. 16p.

(113) WALKER, J. B. Papers in defence of the University of
Tasmania. Hobart, [the Author], 1893-95. 179p.
Contents: A statement of facts; Can we afford it? Is the univers-
ity a luxury? ; The example of the United States.

1895 (114) HUNTER, Sir W. W. and others. State education for the
people in America, Europe, India and Australia, with papers on
the education of women, technical instruction, and payment by
results. Syracuse, NY, Bardeen, 1895. 184p.

(115) WEIGALL, M. How shall I prepare my little boy for school?
Melb, Melville, Mullen & Slade, 1895. 32p.

1896 (116) BAKER, B. A. The education question. Adel, Hussey &
Gillingham, 1896. 12p.

(117) CAMPBELL, C. History of public education in Victoria.
Melb, Melville, Mullen & Slade, 1896. 20p.

(118) HARRIS, J. Education Act of Victoria, and its remedy, by
a miner evangelist. Melb, J. Harrison, 1896. 66p.

1897 (119) BRIDGES, F. Education in New South Wales. [Syd, Department of Public Instruction, 1897?]. 6p.

1898 (120) CAMPBELL, C. The education question: its present
position and the Roman Catholic claims. Melb, Melville, Mullen
& Slade, 1898. 16p.

(121) CAMPBELL, F. A. Some facts, opinions and conclusions
about technical education. Melb, Vic Printing Works, 1898. 24p.

(122) MEREWETHER, F. L. S. University of Sydney; reminiscences. [Syd, the Author, 1898?]. 4p.

1899 (123) CAMPBELL, F. A. The industrial training of the people a
problem; lecture delivered under the auspices of the Victorian
Association for the Promotion of Technical Education. Melb,
A. & W. Bruce, 1899. 8p.

(124) MUSKETT, P. E. The diet of Australian school children;
and, Technical education. Melb, G. Robertson, 1899. 179p.

2   20th Century Views of 19th Century Education

Works by later writers on 19th century education in Australia. Includes histories of education concerned principally with the 19th century.

1917 (125) SMITH, S. H.   A brief history of education in Australia, 1788-1884. Syd, A & R, 1917. 86p.

1922 (126) SWEETMAN, E., Long, C. R. and Smyth, J.   A history of state education in Victoria. Melb, Education Dept, 1922. 320p.

1925 (127) SMITH, S. H. and Spaull, G. P.   History of education in New South Wales, 1788-1925. Syd, Philip, 1925. 267p.

1926 (128) RANKIN, D. H.   The history of the development of education in Western Australia, 1829-1923. Perth, Carrolls, 1926. 272p.

1927 (129) SMEATON, T. H.   Education in South Australia from 1836 to 1927. Adel, Rigby, 1927. 137p.

1936 (130) BRAND, R. F., editor   One hundred years of education; being a record of the development of the educational system of South Australia, 1836-1936. Adel, Printers Trade School, 1936. 31p.

1938 (131) LINZ, C. C.   The establishment of a national system of education in New South Wales. Melb, MUP, 1938. 84p. (ACER Educational Research Series, no 51).

1939 (132) PESCOTT, E. E.   James Bonwick: a writer of school books and histories, with a bibliography of his writings. Melb, H. A. Evans, 1939. 43p.
'To James Bonwick ... falls the great honour of having introduced the first Australian-published school books for Australian children'. (introduction).

(133) RANKIN, D. H.   The history of the development of education in Victoria, 1836-1936; the first centenary of educational effort. Melb, Arrow Printery, 1939. 338p.

(134) SWEETMAN, E.   Victoria's first public educationist: [Rev James Forbes]. Melb, MUP, 1939, 123p. (ACER Educational Research Series, no 55).
Forbes was founder of Chalmers Free Church School, which became the Melbourne Academy, which later grew into the Scotch College.

1940 (135) SWEETMAN, E. The educational activities in Victoria of the Rt Hon H. C. E. Childers. Melb, MUP, 1940. 140p. (ACER Educational Research Series, no 58).
Childers was in Victoria between 1850 and 1857. He was one of the national Commissioners of Education and was the founder of the University of Melbourne.

1955 (136) WYETH, E. R. Education in Queensland; a history of education in Queensland and in the Moreton Bay district of New South Wales. Melb, ACER, 1955. (Educational Research Series, no. 67).

1957 (137) GRIFFITHS, D. S. , editor. Documents on the establishment of education in New South Wales, 1789-1880. Melb, ACER, 1957. 221p. (Educational Research Series, no 70).

1958 (138) AUSTIN, A. G. George William Rusden and national education in Australia, 1849-62. Melb, MUP, 1958. 159p.

1961 (139) AUSTIN, A. G. Australian education, 1788-1900: church, state and public education in colonial Australia. Melb, Pitman, 1961. 292p.

1962 (140) KELLEHER, J. M. Roman fever; a story of the struggle by the Catholic people of New South Wales to remedy the injustice caused by the Education Acts of 1866 and 1880. Syd, Catholic Press Newspaper Co, 1962. 139p.

1963 (141) AUSTIN, A. G. , editor. Select documents in Australian education, 1788-1900. Melb, Pitman, 1963. 299p. (Education in Australia Series).

1964 (142) DOW, G. M. George Higinbotham: church and state. Melb, Pitman, 1964. 227p. (Education in Australia Series).
Higinbotham was Chief Justice in Victoria, 1886-92, and Chairman of 1866 Royal Commission on Education in Victoria.

(143) HOWELL, P. A. Thomas Arnold the younger in Van Diemen's Land. Hobart, Tasmanian Historical Research Assn, 1964. 69p.
Arnold was Inspector of Schools in Tasmania, 1850-56.

1965 (144) BARCAN, A. A short history of education in NSW. Syd, Martindale Press, 1965. 352p.

1966 (145) NEW South Wales Archives Authority. Record groups NBNE and NDSE: the administration of education under two boards, 1848-66. A preliminary inventory of the records of the Board of National Education and the Denominational School Board. Syd, 1966. 106p.

1968 (146) GOODMAN, R. D. Secondary education in Queensland, 1860-1960. Canb, ANU Press, 1968. 405p.

(147) TREGENZA, J. Professor of democracy; the life of Charles Henry Pearson, 1830-94. Melb, MUP, 1968. 295p.
Pearson was Minister for Public Instruction in Victoria, 1886-90.

1969 (148) MADDERN, I. T. A short history of state education in Victoria. Morwell, Vic, [the Author?], 1969. 24p.

(149) TURNEY, C. , editor. Pioneers of Australian education; a study of the development of education in New South Wales in the nineteenth century. Syd, Syd Univ Press, 1969. 277p.

1971 (150) CLEVERLEY, J. F. The first generation; school and society in early Australia. Syd, Syd Univ Press, 1971. 176p.

(151) MOSSENSON, D. State education in Western Australia, 1829-1960. Nedlands, WA, Univ of WA, 1971. 202p.

1972 (152) GRUNDY, D. Secular, compulsory and free; the Education Act of 1872. Carlton, Vic, MUP, 1972. 103p. (Second Century in Australian Education, no 5).

(153) HYAMS, B. K. and Bessant, B. Schools for the people? An introduction to the history of state education in Australia. Camberwell, Vic, Longmans, 1972. 195p.

B   Australian Education in the 20th Century

1 Educational Aims and Policies

(i) Criticism, Evaluation, Philosophy, Principles, Theories

This section includes general works about education. These cover philosophy of education, educational theories and principles, criticism and evaluation. Entries under Research (pages 74-76) also contain some entries relevant to this section.

1924 (154) COLE, P. R. Studies in the history of education. Syd, Teachers College Press, 1924. 96p.

1927 (155) BROWN, G. S. Education in Australia; a comparative study of the educational system of the six Australian states. Lond, Macmillan, 1927. 482p.
Contents: New South Wales by P. R. Cole; Victoria by G. S. Browne; South Australia by A. J. Schulz; Queensland by F. C. Thompson; Western Australia by W. Clubb; Tasmania by J. A. Johnson; Educational statistics.

1928 (156) INSTITUTE of Inspectors of Schools of New South Wales. Educational efficiency. Syd, G. B. Phillip, 1928. 316p. (Publication no 2).

1932 (157) AUSTRALIAN educational studies (first series) by K. S. Cunningham and others. Melb, MUP, 1932. 125p. (ACER Educational Research Series, no 14).
Contents: The length of the teacher's professional life by K. S. Cunningham; An experiment in the teaching of reading comprehension by G. Limb and H. T. Parker; Standardised tests of teaching ability by P. R. Cole and R. K. Whately; Problem children in Melbourne schools by K. S. Cunningham; Crippled children in Tasmania by H. T. Parker; The story of an Australian nursery school by M. V. Gutteridge.

(158) MACKIE, A. Studies in education. Syd, Teachers College Press, 1932. 134p.
Has chapters on the meaning, study and purpose of education, the school system, teaching.

1936 (159) DUNCAN, W. G. K., editor. Educating a democracy: papers read at the Conference of the Australian Institute of Political Science, Canberra, 1936. Syd, A & R, 1936. 189p.

1937 (160) PORTUS, G. V. Free, compulsory and secular: a critical estimate of Australian education. Lond, OUP, 1937. 71p.

1938 (161) CAMPBELL, A. E. and Bailey, C. L., editors. Modern trends in education: the proceedings of the New Education Fellowship Conference held in New Zealand in July 1937. Wellington, NZ, Whitcombe & Tombs, 1938. 528p.

(162) NEW Education Fellowship Conference, Eighth, Australian, 1 August to 20 September 1937. Education for complete living: the .... challenge of today. The proceedings of the .... conference, edited by K. S. Cunningham assisted by W. C. Radford. Melb, MUP, for ACER, 1938. 712p.

1939 (163) BIAGGINI, E. G. Education and society. Lond, Hutchinson's Scientific & Technical Publications, 1939. 233p.

(164) BOARD, P. Whither education? Syd, A & R, 1939. 38p.

(165) DARLING, Sir J. R. Growing up. Corio, Vic, Geelong Grammar School, 1939. 12p.

1940 (166) AUSTRALIAN educational studies (second series). Melb, MUP, 1940. 208p. (ACER Educational Research Series, no 59). Contents: Education for uncertainty by J. D. G. Medley; Some aspects of the educational opportunity in South Australia by J. A. LaNauze; Art in elementary and secondary school education by R. T. Crosthwaite; Impressions and experiments of an Australian teacher by H. C. Robinson; The education of Nazi women by A. Dane.

(167) CASEY of Berwick, Richard Gardiner Casey, baron. Great opportunities; broadcast talk, 13 July 1939. Adel, Young Liberal League, 1940. 7p. (Educational Pamphlets, no 27).

1941 (168) ASHBY, E. Are we educated? Syd, Consolidated Press, 1941. 56p.

(169) HOGG, G. H. Education in relation to political control and religion; [an address]. Launceston, Tas, The Examiner, 1941. 8p.

(170) RANKIN, D. H. The philosophy of Australian education. Melb, Arrow Printery, 1941. 296p.

1943 (171) BROKEN HILL Education Conference, Broken Hill, 1943. A report of the speeches delivered. Melb, Advisory Council of the Conference and ACER, 1943. 128p.

(172) CARSON-Cooling, G. Education in post-war reconstruction. Brisb, the Author, Brisb Grammar School, 1943. 66p. 'The criticisms and proposals ... are offered because ... I feel that education in its present form has failed in its duty to humanity' (preface).

(173) LA NAUZE, J. A. Education for some. Melb, ACER, 1943. 32p. (Future of Education Series, no 3).

(174) MEDLEY, J. D. G. Education for democracy. Melb, ACER, 1943. 31p. (Future of Education Series, no 1).

(175) NEW Education Fellowship, Queensland Section. Education and world reconstruction: report of Education Conference, Brisbane, 16-19 August 1943. Brisb, 1943. 112p.

(176) A PLAN for Australia. Melb, ACER, 1943. 32p. (Future of Education Series, no 2).

(177) PRICE, A. G. Australian education in a changing world, with particular reference to Federal aspects; an address given before the Workers Educational Association, University of Adelaide. Adel, Advertiser Printing Office, 1943. 16p.

1944 (178) BIAGGINI, E. G. A new world for education. Adel, WEA (SA), 1944. 40p.

(179) BURGMANN, E. H., Bishop of Goulburn. The education of an Australian. Syd, A & R, 1944. 101p.
'An autobiographical account of the author's early years embodying his theories of education'.

(180) DRURY, A. N. Youth sees tomorrow; the new education for living. Melb, Whitcombe & Tombs, 1944. 64p.

(181) KING, A. Everyone's business. Melb, OUP, 1944. 96p.

(182) LATHAM, Sir J. G.Education and war. Melb, MUP, 1944. 20p. (John Smyth Memorial Lecture, 1943).

(183) MEDLEY, J. D. G. Education and reconstruction. Melb, MUP, 1944. 26p. (Realities of Reconstruction, no 10).

(184) NEW Education Fellowship, Queensland Section. Education as a community service; report of Education Conference, Brisbane, 21-24 August 1944. Brisb, 1944. 116p.

(185) STEWART, J. I. M. Educating the emotions. Adel, NEF (SA) 1944. 23p.

(186) STEWART, J. I. M. Study and experience; [an address]. Adel, WEA Press, 1944. 23p.

1945 (187) DICKINSON, S. R. The essential basis of a new order: or, The education of the young as social units. Melb, the Author, 1945. 19p.

(188) NEW Education Fellowship. South Australian Section. Education for tomorrow now. Adel, Hunken, Ellis & King, 1945. 64p.

1946 (189) ASHBY, E. Challenge to education. Syd, A & R, 1946. 139p.

(190) BEST, R. J., editor. Education for international understanding; selected addresses to the International Education Conference held in Australia from 31 August to 12 October 1946. Adel, NEF, 1948. 376p.

(191) FISHER, A. G. B. Education and economic change. Adel, WEA Press, 1946. 36p.

(192) HARRIS, H. L. Doing our best for our children. Syd, A & R, 1946. 111p.
Written to 'assist parents to discharge their own responsibilities ... and to convince the community that a responsibility for the welfare of youth has in fact been incurred'.

(193) HENDERSON, N. K. Your child and his future; education and opportunities in Australia. Melb, Research Group, Left Book Club of Vic, 1946. 48p. (Left Book Club of Victoria Research Group Pamphlet, no 10).

(194) VICTORIAN Assistant Masters Association. As the teacher sees it; a statement of educational beliefs. Melb, the Association, 1946. 24p.

1947 (195) AUSTRALIAN Council for Educational Research. Comments and suggestions on educational statistics compiled by education departments in Australia. Melb, 1947. 47 leaves.

(196) BROWN, H. A. Some reflections on the philosophy of education and our national schools. Melb, the Author, 1947. 120p.
'Intended for those about to enter the teaching profession' (introduction).

1948 (197) CURRIE, G. A. A scientist in search of education. Brisb, Univ of Qld, 1948. 36p. (John Murtagh Macrossan Lectures, 1947).

(198) LOWE, Sir C. J. A literate democracy; being an address delivered at the 19th annual commencement ceremony of the Canberra University College on 30 April 1948. Canb, Canb Univ College, 1948. 16p.

(199) WILCHER, L. Education: press: radio. Melb, Cheshire, 1948. 110p.

1949 (200) SOME statistical data on education in Australia. Melb, ACER, 1949. 12 leaves. (Information Bulletin, no 18).
Contents: Schools, students, teachers, 1946; Average age in grade: comparison; Age at leaving school, etc; Some statistics on teachers.

1951 (201) AUSTRALIAN National Advisory Committee for Unesco. Compulsory education in Australia; a study. Paris, Unesco, 1951. 189p. (Unesco Studies on Compulsory Education, no 3).
Second edition 1962.

1953 (202) RATING of American comics. Melb, ACER, 1953. 6 leaves. (Information Bulletin no 26).
Findings of the Cincinnati (USA) Committee.

(203) AUSTIN, M. N. The presence of the past; an inaugural address delivered on 17 July 1952. Perth, Univ of WA, 1953. 19p.

1955 (204) BUTTS, R. F. Assumptions underlying Australian education. Melb, ACER, 1955. 93p.
Reprinted 1955 by Teachers College, Columbia University, New York, USA.

(205) SANDERS, G. Teacher, school and university; [an address]. Nedlands, WA, Univ of WA Publications Committee, 1955. 24p.

1957 (206) MONAHAN, B. W. Aims of education. Syd, Tidal Publications, 1957. 48p.
Bound with 'Why I am a social creditor'.

(207) PHILLIPS, F. G. School is out. Syd, A & R, 1957. 191p.
Reminiscences and addresses.

1958 (208) CONFERENCE on Education for Australia's Future, Melbourne, October 10-11 1958. Education for Australia's future; report.
Melb, Assistant Mistresses Assn of Vic, 1958. 88p.

1959 (209) ANDERSON, W. H. The New Education Fellowship in Western Australia; a history written at the request of the WA section of the Fellowship to commemorate 21 years of activity 1938-59. Perth, NEF, 1959. 9p.

(210) GOLLAN, W. E. Education in crisis. Syd, Current Book Distributors, 1959. 48p.

1960 (211) DARLING, J. R. and others. Educational values in a democracy. Melb, Cheshire for the Aust College of Education, 1960. 75p.

(212) NATIONAL Education Conference, Sydney, 1960. Report. Syd, 1960. 15p.
Conference was called by the Australian Council of School Organisations and the Australian Teachers Federation and 'was the largest and most representative delegate conference in Australian history' with more than 3000 delegates attending.

1961 (213) AUSTRALIAN College of Education. The challenge to Australian education: lectures presented at the second annual conference. Melb, 1961. 75p.
Contents: The challenge to education by R. G. Menzies; The qualities and training of teachers by W. H. Frederick; The government of Australian education by A. Barcan; Educational influences outside the school and university by R. B. Madgwick; Tertiary education in Australia by W. J. Weeden.

(214) BRIGGS, A. The map of leaning. Canb, ANU, 1961. 30p.
(ANU Canberra Research Students Association Annual Lecture, 1st, 1960).

(215) CONNELL, W. F. and others. The foundations of education.
Syd, Novak, 1962. 318p.
Second edition published in 1967. Also published by Cresset Press
in 1962.

1962 (216) CLARKE, M. The archaic principle in education. Glasgow,
MacLellan, 1962. 119p.
Discusses the disappearance of the teaching of Greek and Latin in
schools.

(217) DARLING, J. R. The education of a civilized man: a
selection of speeches and sermons. Melb, Cheshire, 1962. 233p.

(218) GIBSON, A. B. Towards an Australian philosophy of education: three lectures. Syd, Dept of Education, 1962. 75p.

1963 (219) AUSTRALIAN College of Education. Educating for tomorrow:
addresses presented to the Fourth Annual Meeting and Conference of
the Australian College of Education held at Perth from 17 to 21 May
1963, by J. R. Darling and others. Melb, Cheshire, 1963. 92p.
Contents: Educating for tomorrow by J. R. Darling; The enlarging
fields of education by H. S. Wyndham; Education in the scientific
age by N. S. Bayliss; Race tensions in Central Africa by E. J. P.
Matthews; Racial tension in Papua New Guinea by D. G. Bettison;
Education for responsible citizens for tomorrow by A. K. Stout and
F. R. Arnott.

(220) AUSTRALIAN Education Council. A statement of some needs
of Australian education. Syd, NSW Parent Teacher Education
Council, 1963. 7p.
Revised Edition 1963. 3rd edition 1970 entitled 'Nationwide survey
of educational needs'.

(221) AUSTRALIAN education today: [articles reprinted from
Education News]. Syd, Commonwealth Office of Education, 1963.
107p.

(222) CUNNINGHAM, K. S. and Radford, W. C. Training the
administrator; a study with special reference to education.
Hawthorn, Vic, ACER, 1963. 135p.

(223) HASLUCK, A. Evelyn Hill; a memoir by her daughter.
Melb, Hawthorn Press, 1963. 17p.

(224) PATERSON, J. Education in Australia: students report.
Melb, Melb Univ Students Representative Council, 1963. 40p.

1964 (225) AUSTRALIAN College of Education. Australia and its
neighbours; an educational aspect. Melb, Cheshire for the Aust
College of Education, 1965. 165p.
Papers from the 5th Annual Conference, Canberra, 1964.
Contents: Australia and its neighbours by P. Hasluck; The
educational problems of India by B. K. Massand; Australia and
Asia: some comparisons in relation to education by W. D. Borrie;
The resources of Australia by C. S. Christian; Problems of
agricultural education in South East Asia by H. C. Forster; The

role of radio and television by F. Watts; Teaching English as a foreign language by A. P. Anderson; What are we doing for foreign students? by A. F. Tylee, G. Caiger and S. W. Kurrle; The services of Australians overseas by J. J. Pratt.

(226) AUSTRALIAN Congress for International Co-operation and Disarmament, Sydney 1964. Educationists Conference. Mankind owes the child the best it has to give. Syd, 1964. 10p.

(227) BECK, F. A. G. Greek education, 450-350 BC. Lond, Methuen, 1964. 381p.

(228) CAMPION, Mary, Sister. The two halves of our future. Adel, Service to Youth Council, 1964. 12p.
Address delivered to annual general meeting of the Service to Youth Council Inc, 22 June 1964.

(229) COWAN, R. W. T., editor. Education for Australians; a symposium. Melb, Cheshire, 1964. 298p.

(230) READ, Sir H. E. Art and education. Melb, Cheshire, 1964. 74p.

1965 (231) AUSTRALIA. Commonwealth Office of Education. Education in Australia. Syd, 1965. 33p.

(232) CITIZENS Education Campaign. Forum on education; is there a crisis? Monash University, Monday 27 September 1965. Clayton, Vic, 1965. 65p.
'Teach-in' sponsored by the Student Councils of Monash University, the University of Melbourne and Royal Melbourne Institute of Technology, and the Citizens Education Campaign.

(233) NATIONAL Union of Australian University Students. Education; policy as adopted at Perth, February 1965. [Melb?, 1965]. 66p.

(234) RADFORD, W. C. Education in Australia for personal and national development. Syd, Mackie Memorial Trust Committee, 1965. 30p. (Second Mackie Lecture, Sydney, 1965).

1966 (235) AUSTIN, M. N. An ignorant man thinking; essays and addresses. Nedlands, WA, Univ of WA Press, 1966. 254p.

(236) AUSTRALIA. Commonwealth Office of Education. Education in Australia; developments during 1965, report presented at the XXIXth International Conference on Public Education, Geneva, 1966. [Syd, 1966]. 17p.

(237) AUSTRALIAN Council for Educational Research. Variations in Australian education; some interstate differences in practices and organisations in Australian education with particular reference to transfer during primary and secondary schooling. Hawthorn, Vic, 1966. 47p.
Report prepared for the Australian College of Education.

(238) AUSTRALIAN National University. School of General
Studies. Students Association. Education teach-in, 26 April 1966;
abridged speeches. Canb, 1966. 36p.

(239) CONNELL, W. F., Debus, R. L. and Niblett, W. R., editors.
Readings in the foundation of education. Syd, Novak, 1966. 414p.
Published by Routledge & Kegan Paul, London in 1967.
Contains extracts from books and articles dealing with basic issues
in education.

(240) HUNT, M. W. The crisis in education; a student report.
Perth, Guild of Undergraduates, Univ of WA, 1966. 21p.

(241) MACKIE, M. Education in the inquiring society; an
introduction to the philosophy of education. Hawthorn, Vic, ACER,
1966. 147p.

(242) SEMINAR on Education and International Cooperation, Grafton,
NSW, 1966. Proceedings of the Australian UNESCO Seminar. Syd,
Aust National Advisory Committee for UNESCO, 1966. 73p.

1967 (243) CATHIE, I. The crisis in Australian education. Melb,
Cheshire. 1967. 152p.

(244) MADDERN, I. T. A new concept of education. Morwell,
Vic, Morwell High School, 1967. 20p.

(245) PRATT, J. J. Some thoughts on Australian education:
planning for an increased commitment; address, University of NSW,
14 July 1967. Syd, Univ of NSW, 1967. 13p.

(246) SCHOOLS, colleges and society. Carlton, Vic, Australian
College of Education, 1967. 105p.
Papers presented at the 8th Annual Conference, 1967 of the
Australian College of Education.
Contents: Test and contest by C. E. Moorhouse; Educational
planning, benefits and dangers by P. W. Hughes; Schools, society
and development in New Guinea by H. R. McKinnon; The community
and decentralisation of higher education by L. N. Short; The social
function of the faculty of arts by R. St C. Johnson; The social
function of schools and colleges by Sister M. Campion; The
social function of a rural independent boarding school by D. Evers;
The passing of 'progressive' education in the USA by L. C. D. Kemp;
Religious education in schools and colleges by T. H. Timpson.

(247) VICTORIAN Council of School Organizations. The problems
of inner-suburban schools; a report of a seminar. Melb, 1967.
15p.
Addendum to appendix 2. 3 leaves.

(248) WARK, I. W. Education: how much, quantity and quality?
Hobart, Adult Education Board, 1967. 15p. (Sir John Morris
Memorial Lecture 1967).

1968 (249) BIGGS, J. B. Information and human learning. Melb, Cassell,
1968. 135p.

(250) MACKIE, M. Educative teaching. Syd, A & R, 1968. 297p. 'A discussion of some of the problems of education with special reference to Australian secondary schools'.

(251) McLAREN, J. Our troubled schools. Melb, Cheshire, 1968. 275p.

(252) PARTRIDGE, P. H. Society, schools and progress in Australia. Oxford, Pergamon Press, 1968. 246p. (Commonwealth and International Library Education and Educational Research Division).

(253) PHILP, H. Factors affecting the educability of children. Hawthorn, Vic, ACER, 1968. 25p. (Information Bulletin, no 49).

(254) RADFORD, W. C. Education and training in Australia. Melb, [ACER?], 1968. 21p. (Duke of Edinburgh's Commonwealth Study Conference, 3rd, Melbourne, 1968. Background Paper 9).

(255) WALKER, W. G. Education in the organizational society; the role of a faculty of education. Armidale, NSW, Univ of New England, 1968. 27p. (Inaugural Public Lecture).

1969 (256) CHAMPION, R. A. Learning and activation. Syd, Wiley, 1969. 136p.

(257) COMMUNIST Party of Australia. Public education in a modern world. Syd, D. B. Young, 1969. 12p.

(258) FENLEY, W. J. , editor. Education in the 1970's and 1980's; continuity and change in Australian education. Syd, Univ of Syd, Dept of Education, 1969. 179p.

(259) FRASER, J. M. Speech delivered at the National Education Conference, Adelaide, 28 June 1969. [Canb?, the Author?], 1969. 18 leaves.

(260) HOWIE, G. Educational theory and practice in St Augustine. Lond, Routledge & Kegan Paul, 1969. 344p.

(261) McLEAN, D. , editor. It's people that matter: education for social change. Syd, A & R, 1969. 352p. A collection of essays. 'The purpose of this book is to assist the changes now affecting certain Australian attitudes towards education and life'.

(262) NATIONAL Education Conference, Adelaide, 1969. Education down under; a report. Melb, Aust Council of State School Organisations, 1969. 24p. Sponsored by the Australian Council of State School Organisations in association with the Australian Teachers Federation.

(263) NATIONAL Union of Australian University Students. Education Department. Fact sheet in inequalities in Australian education, prepared by T. W. Roper. North Melb, Vic, 1969. 81p.

(264) TURNER, M. L. The development of courses for Australian schools. Hawthorn, Vic, ACER, 1969. 32p. (Quarterly Review of Australian Education, vol 2, no 3).

1970 (265) ARCHDALE, H. E. Girls at school. Syd, Hodder & Stoughton, 1970. 95p.

(266) AUSTRALIA. Department of Education and Science. Education in Australia. Canb, Aust Govt Publishing Service, 1970. 49p.

(267) BASSETT, G. W. Planning in Australian education; report of a seminar on educational planning. Hawthorn, Vic, ACER, 1970. 453p.
Report on the National Seminar on Educational Planning conducted in Canberra under the auspices of the Australian National Advisory Committee for UNESCO in September 1968.

(268) FENSHAM, P. J., editor. Rights and inequality in Australian education. Melb, Cheshire, 1970. 227p.

(269) KATZ, F. M. and Browne, R. K., editors. Sociology of education; a book of readings pertinent to the Australian education system. South Melb, Macmillan, 1970. 405p.

(270) MUSGRAVE, P. W., editor. Sociology, history and education; a reader. Lond, Methuen, 1970. 301p.

(271) ROPER, T. W. Myth of equality. Melb, NUAUS, 1970. 91p.

(272) WALKER, W. G. Theory and practice in educational administration. St Lucia, Qld, Univ of Qld Press, 1970. 214p.

1971 (273) AUSTRALIAN College of Education. Planning for effective education: papers given at the Twelfth Annual Conference, Perth, May 1971 . Melb, 1971. 187p.
Contents: People, policies and planning by W. C. Radford; Planning for effective education by R. T. Fitzgerald; Education for administration by W. G. Walker and A. R. Thomas; Helping the teacher through system administration by J. G. Williams; The school and its locality by C. J. Balmer; Creating classroom climate by influencing norms by K. D. Pearson; Planning education and training for industry's needs by R. V. Lawson; Technology, tradition and tabu; the planning of tertiary technical education in New Guinea by P. B. Botsman; Computers in Australian education by B. S. Abrahams; Unit progress -an attempt to cater for individual differences by M. Philson; The generation gap in administrative structures by H. Beare; Education for administration is not enough by K. R. Lamacraft; Planning for effective education by D. A. Jecks; The use of mathematical models as an aid to effective planning in education by H. W. S. Philp and J. N. Johnstone.

(274) AUSTRALIAN College of Education. Victorian Chapter. Sub Committee on the Education of Girls. The education of girls and the employment of women. [Melb] , 1971. 67p. (Convener: W. A. F. Lang).

(275) KEMP, D. Introduction to education. Syd, Novak, 1971. 230p.

(276) MACLAINE, A. G. and Selby Smith, R. , editors. Fundamental issues in Australian education; a book of readings. Syd, Novak, 1971. 435p.

(277) PHILLIPS, D. C. Theories, values and education. Melb, MUP, 1971. 94p. (Second Century in Australian Education Series, no 2).

(278) ROBERTS, M. D. Some problems of education in a competitive society. Syd, Ascham Parents Assn, 1971. 12p.

1972 (279) BECKENHAM, P. W. J. H. Sensitivity and the twentieth century, being the NSW Chapter Chairman's address 10 July 1971. Manly, NSW, Aust College of Education, NSW Chapter, 1971. 11 leaves.

(280) BOWEN, J. E. A history of Western education. Volume 1: The ancient world, Orient and Mediterranean, 2000 BC - AD 1054. Lond, Methuen, 1972. 414p.

(281) BROWN, D. W. F. Putting minds to work; an introduction to modern pedagogy. Syd, Wiley, 1972. 285p.

(282) CLEVERLEY, J. F. and Lawry, J. , editors. Australian education in the twentieth century; studies in the development of state education. Camberwell, Vic, Longman, 1972. 209p. Contents: Understanding Australian education 1901-14 by J. Lawry; Continuity and change in the public primary schools by C. Turney; The state primary school teacher between the wars by J. Cleverley; Ideas, theories and assumptions in Australian education by K. S. Cunningham; The emergence of state secondary education by B. Bessant; The Commonwealth and education 1901-69 by E. Bowker; The transition in Australian education 1939-67 by A. Barcan.

(283) LAWSON, M. D. and Petersen, R. C. Progressive education; an introduction. Syd, A & R, 1972. 126p.

(284) WALKER, W. G. , editor. School, college and university; the administration of education in Australia. St Lucia, Qld, Univ of Qld Press, 1972. 264p. Contents: The growth of Federal participation in Australian education by Z. Cowen; Bureaucracy in educational organization: an overview by W. G. Walker; The government school by A. W. Jones; The university by A. J. Davies; Communication in educational organization: an overview by A. R. Crane; The government

school by P. W. Hughes; The independent school by M. A. Howell;
The university by R. McCaig; Occupations, personnel and careers
in education: an overview by R. O. Carlson; The government
school by I. F. Vacchini; The university by G. W. Bassett; The
preparation of educational administrators: an overview by G. W.
Muir; The Victorian government school by W. B. Russell; The
NSW government school by D. A. Buchanan; The independent
school by A. H. Cash; The governance of education: policy making
and local education authorities in England by G. Baron.

(ii) Religion in Education

See subject index for other works.

1900 (285) BERRY, Rev D. M. Rome; the enemy of national education.
Melb, Evangelical Church Assn, [190?]. 19p.

(286) TAYLOR, A. J. Free education and the Churches. Hobart,
Tasmanian News, 1900. 4p.

1907 (287) HIGGINS, J. The Church and education. Melb, Catholic
Truth Society, 1907. 31p.

1930 (288) CORRIGAN, U. Catholic education in New South Wales.
Syd, A & R, 1930. 151p.

1943 (289) O'BRIEN, Rev E. and others. Religion in education; five
addresses delivered before the New Education Fellowship, NSW.
Syd, Tomalin and Wigmore, 1943. 56p.

1945 (290) DOWN, H. P. Not kings, but men. Melb, R & M, 1945.
142p.
Addresses with a religious basis by the headmaster of a Melbourne
school.

1949 (291) CATHOLIC Action. Australian National Secretariat.
Christian education in a democratic community; published with
the authority of the archbishops and bishops of the Catholic Church
in Australia. Melb, 1949. 18p.

1958 (292) COUNCIL for Christian Education in Schools, Victoria.
The agreed syllabus as approved by all the constituent churches
of the Council ... primary schools, grades 1 to 6 ... prepared
under the authority of the Education, Religious Instruction, Act
1950 and regulations. Melb, 1958. 19 p.

1959 (293) FOGARTY, R. Catholic education in Australia, 1806-1950.
Melb, MUP, 1959. 2 vols.

1960 (294) COUNCIL for Christian Education in Schools, Victoria. The
agreed syllabus of religious instruction for secondary schools, as
adopted by the Council ... and approved by all the constituent
churches: forms 1 to 6 ... prepared in accordance with the
Education, Religious Instruction, Act 1950 and regulations. Melb,
[1960?]. 64p.

(295) SANTAMARIA, B. A. Equality in education; [an address].
Melb, Inst of Social Order, 1960. 30p.

1961 (296) NEW South Wales Humanist Society. Report of the sub-
committee on religious education. Syd, 1961. 12p.

1963 (297) ROMAN Catholic Church in Australia. Archdiocese of
Melbourne. Catholic education; the challenge of the rising
generations must be met. Melb, 1963. 6p.

(298) ROMAN Catholic Church in Australia. Archdiocese of
Melbourne. Catholic education; past, present, future. Melb,
1963. 15p.

1966 (299) BOURKE, D. F. , compiler. Catholic education; some
statistics. Surry Hills, NSW, Catholic Press Newspaper Co, 1966.
8p.

(300) CONFERENCE on Theological Education, Morpeth 1966. The
Morpeth papers. Syd, Aust Council of Churches for the Ecumenical
Book and Documents Club, 1966. 72p.
Conference convened by J. A. G. Housden, Bishop of Newcastle.

1967 (301) CONFERENCE on Religious Education, Canberra Grammar
School 1967. Proceedings of the Conference on Religious Education
organised by the Headmaster's Conference of the Independent Schools
of Australia. Canb, 1967. 62p.

(302) SPEEDY, G. Guide to adult study. Melb, Joint Board of
Christian Education of Aust and NZ, 1967. 32p.
Notes for teaching religious education to adults.

(303) SPEEDY, G. Team teaching. Melb, Joint Board of Christian
Education of Aust and NZ 1967. 32p.
Team teaching methods applied to religious education.

1968 (304) SEMINAR on Religion in Independent Schools, Kirribilli,
NSW, 15 and 16 March 1968. Syd, Teachers Guild of NSW, 1968.
44p.

1969 (305) AUSTRALIAN Frontier. Religious instruction in state
schools. Canb, 1969. 28p. (Australian Frontier Consultation
Report).

1970 (306) AUSTRALIAN Frontier. The role of the church in education
today. Malvern, Vic, 1970. 35p.

(307) MELBOURNE Catholic Education Board. How do you see
the future of Catholic education? Fitzroy, Vic, 1970. 7p.

(308) SELLECK, R. J. W. Crudden: the reluctant rebel. Melb,
Heinemann Educational, 1970. 59p.

(309) TASMANIAN Catholic Education Conference, Hobart 1970.
[Papers presented. Hobart, Tas Catholic Education Office, 1970].
2 vols.

1971 (310) BRENNAN, N. Indoctrination or education? Melb, [Aust Catholic Truth Society, 1971]. 30p.

(311) BRASSIL, J. T. C. and Daffey, B. M. The Catholic school in a pluralist society; one hundred years of Catholic education. Melb, Catholic Education Office, [1971]. 150p.

(312) THE FUTURE for a school system; a plan for the Archdiocese of Melbourne. Report of the Catholic Education Office to the Melbourne Catholic Education Board, 13 October 1971. Melb, Advocate Press, 1971. 36p.

(313) NATIONAL Summer School on Religion, 1st, Australian National University, 1970. Moral education and the formation of attitudes: papers arising from the school, edited by J. Nurser. Canb, Centre for Continuing Education, ANU, 1971. 71p.

(314) 'SOUTHERN Cross' on education: a chronological collection of excerpts from the South Australian Catholic weekly from vol 1 no 1 [1889] through 1949. Adel, Wattle Park Teachers College, 1971. 3 vols.

1972 (315) GILL, P., editor. Catholic education: where is it going? North Melb, Cassell Aust, 1972. 175p.

(316) O'DONOGHUE, M. X. Mother Vincent Whitty; women and education in a masculine society. Melb, MUP, 1972. 200p.

(317) TURNER, N. Sinews of sectarian warfare? State aid in New South Wales, 1836-62. Canb, ANU Press, 1972. 272p.

(iii) Comparative Education

Australian views of overseas education, and some visitors' views of Australian education.

1905 (318) ROE, R. H. The growth of universities in America, with a note on university extension in Queensland. Brisb, Diddams, 1905. 19p.
Presidential address to the Standing Committee of the Queensland University Extension Movement, May 1905.

1923 (319) HANSEN, M. P. Report on systems of accrediting schools in the United States of America. Melb, Melb Univ, 1923. 66p.

1924 (320) TATE, F. Some lessons from rural Denmark; being results of observations made during an official visit to Europe in 1923. Melb, Education Dept, 1924. 83p.

1930 (321) CUNNINGHAM, K. S. and Phillips, G. E. Some aspects of education in the United States of America. Melb, MUP, 1930. 104p. (ACER Educational Research Series, no 2).

1932 (322) BROWNE, G. S. The case for curriculum revision; being a
report submitted to the Director of Education, Victoria as the result
of observations in Great Britain and America. Melb, MUP, 1932.
(ACER Educational Research Series, no 8).

1933 (323) CANNON, J. G. Comments on education in the United States
of America and Victoria, Australia. Melb, MUP, 1933. 58p.
(ACER Educational Research Series, no 18).

(324) McRAE, C. R. An Australian looks at American schools.
Melb, MUP, 1933. 76p. (ACER Educational Research Series,
no 20).

1934 (325) CUNNINGHAM, K. S. Educational observations and reflections, ,
being some comments on present day education in United States,
England, and Australia. Melb, MUP, 1934. 98p. (ACER
Educational Research Series, no 24).

(326) WYNDHAM, H. S. Ability grouping; recent developments
in methods of class-grouping in the elementary schools of the
United States. Melb, MUP, 1934. 248p. (ACER Educational
Research Series, no 31).

1935 (327) MANN, C. W. Education in Fiji. Melb, MUP, 1935. 146p.
(ACER Educational Research Series, no 33).

(328) MOLESWORTH, B. H. Adult education in America and England.
Melb, MUP, 1935. 72p. (ACER Educational Research Series, no 36).

(329) PARKER, H. T. The background of American education, as an.
Australian sees it. Melb, MUP, 1935. 48p. (ACER Educational
Research Series, no 34).

1936 (330) CRAMER, J. F. Australian schools through American eyes.
Melb, MUP, 1936. 59p. (ACER Educational Research Series,
no 42).

(331) VICTORIA. Education Department. Report on technical
education in other countries, by E. P. Eltham. Melb, 1936. 105p

1937 (332) DRUMMOND, D. H. Report of inquiries made into various
aspects of education during a visit to the United Kingdom, Europe,
the United States of America and Canada, and proceedings of the
1936 New Education Fellowship Conference at Cheltenham, England.
Syd, Govt Pr, 1937. 84p.

(333) ELKIN, A. P. Education of native races in Pacific countries;
report of a conference. Syd, A'sian Medical Pub Co, 1937. 24p.
Published in Oceania vol 7 no 2, p. 145-68, December 1936.

(334) KANDEL, I. L. The strife of tongues. Melb, MUP, 1937.
34p. (John Smyth Memorial Lecture, 1937).

1938 (335) KANDEL, I. L. Impressions of Australian education. Melb,
MUP, 1938. 15p.

(336) KANDEL, I. L. Types of administration with particular reference to the educational systems of Australia and New Zealand. Melb, MUP, 1938. 105p. (NZCER Educational Research Series, no 7).

1939 (337) HOY, A. Libraries in the schools of USA: a report submitted to the Australian Council for Educational Research. [Melb, ACER, 1939?]. 23 leaves.

1941 (338) MAISKY, I. M. Soviet youth; its training and opportunities. Melb, Aust Soviet Friendship League, 1941. 20p.

1944 (339) McRAE, D. Education in the Soviet Union. Melb, Aust Soviet Friendship League, 1944. 40p.

1947 (340) SOME current problems in English education. Melb, ACER, 1947. 12 leaves. (Information Bulletin, no 10).

1948 (341) GRAY, R. K. Physical and health education in the universities and colleges of Canada, the United States of America and Great Britain; abstract of a report compiled during 1948-49-50. Melb, ACER, 1950. 35 leaves. (Information Bulletin, no 20).

(342) HIGHER education for American democracy. Melb, ACER, 1948. 4 leaves. (Information Bulletin no 13).
'Summary of the most important sections' of volume 1 of the Zook Report (1947).

(343) PRYOR, L. J. The emergency teacher training scheme in England. [Melb, 1948?]. 202 leaves.

1949 (344) ROWLAND, E. C. Britain's changing schools, Syd, Boulton Bros, 1949. 68p.

1951 (345) CUNNINGHAM, K. S. , editor. The adjustment of youth; a study of a social problem in the British, American and Australian communities. Melb, MUP for ACER, 1951. 264p.

1954 (346) RADFORD, W. C. A general survey of educational research in the United States of America, Canada, England and Scotland: a report. Melb, ACER, 1954. 48 leaves.

1955 (347) ELTHAM, E. P. Technical and industrial training in Western Europe. Melb, the Author, 1955. 9p.

(348) SANDERS, C. Universities and educational institutions in South East Asia; report on standards. Perth, Univ of WA, 1955. 53p.

1956 (349) CRAMER, J. F. and Browne, G. S. Contemporary education; a comparative study of national systems. NY, Harcourt Brace, 1956. 653p.
Second edition 1965.

1958 (350) BRYAN, H. Report of a visit by Mr Harrison Bryan, James Forsyth Librarian within the University of Queensland, to Great Britain and the United States in the course of study leave, 1957/58. Brisb, Qld Univ Library, 1958. 26p.

(351) POWER, H. A. Report on a visit to Great Britain, Holland and Switzerland during 1958. Melb, Royal Melb Technical College, 1958. 18p.

1959 (352) RUSSELL, D. H. Problems and trends in American education. Brisb,Univ of Qld Press, 1960. 26p. (John Murtagh Macrossan Memorial Lecture, 1959).

(353) VICTORIA. Education Department. Report on technical education and apprenticeship training in some countries overseas, by O. E. Nilsson. Melb, 1959. 206p.

1960 (354) EDUCATION Seminar for the South Pacific, Brisbane, 1959. Report and recommendaticns of the regional education seminar held under South Pacific Commission auspices at the University of Queensland, St Lucia, Brisbane, November 16-27 1959. Noumea, South Pacific Commission, 1960. 24p. (South Pacific Commission Technical Paper, no 133).

1962 (355) JACKSON, R. W. B. Emergent needs in Australian education. Melb, ACER, 1962. 32p.
Australian edition; originally published by the Department of Educational Research, Ontario College of Education, University of Toronto, Canada in 1961.

(356) SHAW, J. H. Observations on community development and adult education in North America; a report on a tour of study made between August and November 1961. Armidale, Dept of Adult Education, Univ of New England, 1962. 60p.

1963 (357) BLOOMFIELD, J. S. Screens and gowns; some aspects of university education overseas. Melb, Cheshire, 1963. 136p.

(358) HADLEY, C. and Kirkwood, R. W. Building schools; joint report following studies in England, Scotland, the USA, New Zealand. Syd, Dept of Public Works, 1963. 59p.

1964 (359) UNESCO. Planning Mission. Education in Northern Rhodesia; a report and recommendations prepared by the Unesco Planning Mission, 28 September - 2 December 1963. Lusaka, Govt Pr, 1964. 121p.
Mission members: W. C. Radford, R. W. McCulloch and E. A. Russell.

1965 (360) AUSTRALIAN College of Education, Conference, 5th, Canberra, 1964. Australia and its neighbours; an educational aspect. Melb, Cheshire for the Aust College of Education, 1965. 165p.
Contents: Australia and its neighbours by P. Hasluck; Educational problems of India by B. K. Massand; Australia and Asia: some

some comparisons in relation to education by W. D. Borrie; The resources of Australia by C. S. Christian; Problems of agricultural education in south-east Asia by H. C. Forster; The role of radio and television by F. Watts; Teaching English as a foreign language by A. P. Anderson; What are we doing for foreign students by S. W. Kurrle, A. F. Tylee and G. Caiger; The services of Australian overseas by J. J. Pratt.

(361) FRASER, S. Chinese Communist education; records of the first decade. Nashville, Tenn, Vanderbilt Univ Press, 1965. 557p.

(362) WILLIAMS, H. S. Some observations on vocational education in the United States of America; a report of a three months study tour in North America on a travel grant from the Carnegie Corporation of New York. Perth, Dept of Education, 1965. 40p.

1966 (363) BRYAN, H. A critical survey of university libraries and librarianship in Great Britain. Adel, Libraries Board of SA, 1966. 255p. (South Australia. Libraries Board. Occasional Papers in Librarianship, no 4).
Thesis for the Diploma of the Library Association of Australia, 1959.

1968 (364) BREWSTER, K. The generation of re-appraisal; American students, 1968. Melb, Australian-American Assn, 1968. 7p. (Latham-Blair Memorial Lecture, no 1).

(365) LEESE, J. English education and Australia. Melb, Cheshire, 1968. 131p.

(366) MILLER, T. W. G., editor. Education in South-East Asia. Syd, Novak, 1968. 298p.
'The primary purpose of this book is to introduce students and others interested in comparative education to the evaluation, structure, problems and prospects of education in the countries situated in the south and east of the Asian mainland and adjacent islands' (foreword).

(367) SELLECK, R. J. W. The new education; the English background, 1870-1914. Melb, Pitman, 1968. 389p. (Education in Australia Series).

1969 (368) AUSTRALIA. Delegation of the Commonwealth Education Conference, Fourth, Lagos, 26 February - 9 March 1968; report of the Australian delegation. Canb, Govt Pr, 1969. 42p. (Parliamentary Paper no 58 of 1968).

(369) CLARK, H. W. Report to the South Australian Institute of Teachers on the Fourth Asian Regional Conference of the World Confederation of the Teaching Profession held in Djakarta, 20-26 April 1969. Adel, SAIT, 1969. 13p.

1970 (370) BASSETT, G. W. Innovation in primary education; a study of recent developments in primary education in England and the USA. Lond, Wiley, 1970. 219p.

(371) KRISTER, S. J. Report of a study tour to examine health
education practice in North America, Europe and Asia. Syd, NSW
Dep of Health, 1970. 67p.

(372) EDGAR, P. and Sims, T. A survey of audio visual facilities
in universities in the USA, Canada, United Kingdom and Australia.
Bundoora, Vic, School of Education, La Trobe Univ, 1970. (Technical Report, no 1). 1 vol (various pagination).

(373) GOODMAN, R. D. and others. Trends in external higher
education; case studies from Australia, Japan, New Zealand and
Western Eruope by R. D. Goodman and others. Honolulu, Hawaii,
East-West Center and Unesco, 1970. 1 vol (various pagination).

1971 (374) JONES, P. E. Comparative education; purpose and method.
St Lucia, Qld, Univ of Qld Press, 1971. 225p.

(375) VICTORIA. Education Department. Educational Facilities
Laboratory. Report of a visit to USA, May/August 1971, by R. G.
Allingham. Melbourne, [1971?]. 31 leaves.

(376) WOOD, J. F. D. Liberal studies in United Kingdom poly-
technics; report on a research project undertaken for the
Commonwealth Advisory Committee on Advanced Education.
Kensington, NSW, Univ of NSW, 1971. 87p.

1972 (377) SELLECK, R. J. W. English primary education and the
progressives, 1914-1939. Lond, Routledge & Kegan Paul, 1972.
204p.

(iv) Economic Aspects of Education

1944 (378) WOOD, G. L. The purchasing power of a pedagogue. Melb,
MUP, 1944. 24p. (Professor Smyth Memorial Lecture, 1944).

1945 (379) STATE expenditure on education in Australia and some overseas
countries. Melb, Vic, ACER, 1945. 10 leaves. (Information Bulletin, no 2).

1960 (380) PARENTS and Friends Federation of Victoria. Submission
to the Hon H. E. Bolte, Premier of Victoria, 20 June 1960. Melb,
1960. 5p.
'The Parents and Friends Federation ... consists of organisations
working in and for Catholic Schools in Victoria'.

1961 (381) HEFFRON, R. J. Submissions on education made to the
Premier's Conference, June 1961. Syd, NSW Parent-Teacher
Education Council, 1961. 11p.
Includes 'Some Aspects of Education', a statement compiled under
the direction of the Australian Education Council, which comprises
the Ministers of Education of all the states of the Commonwealth
of Australia.

(382) O'SULLIVAN, K. Equality in education: who should pay? Melb, Aust Catholic Truth Society, 1961. 32p.

(383) THEOBOLD, M. and Evans, G. Taxation and the student; a statement of the policy of the National Union of Australian University Students on those aspects of the taxation legislation of the Commonwealth of Australia which pertain to tertiary students. Melb, NUAUS, 1961. 21p.

1962 (384) KARMEL, P. H. Some economic aspects of education. Melb, Cheshire for the Aust College of Education, 1962. 25p. (Buntine Oration, 1962).

(385) PARENTS and Friends Federation of Victoria. Submission to the Hon H. E. Bolte by a deputation. Melb, 1962. 4p. See note under entry 380, page 35.

1963 (386) STATE aid Goulburn and after. Syd, [1963?] 15p. (Suhard Papers. Matters for Debate, no 1).

1964 (387) BAKER, H. W. Australian church schools and state aid. Parramatta, NSW, the Author, 1964. 12p.

(388) CARNIE, A. A. Public funds and private schools. Hope Valley, SA Humanist Society, 1964. 8p.

(389) GOLLAN, W. E. State aid for education; a current mischief. Syd, Current Book Distributors, 1964. 15p.

(390) MacLAURIN, E. C. B. State aid for non-state schools; some points worth considering. Syd, Anglican Press, 1964. 11p.

(391) NATIONAL Union of Australian University Students. Taxation and the student; a brief concerning education and the income tax laws. Melb, 1964. 21p.

1965 (392) ADISESHIAH, M. S. The relationship of education to economic development. Port Moresby, Dept of Education, 1965. 20p. (Camilla Wedgwood Memorial Lecture, 6th, 1965).

(393) AUSTRALIAN Council of State School Organisations. 7000 Australian parent organisations say state aid for non-state schools is dangerous. Melb, 1965. 15p.

1966 (394) ALBINSKI, H. S. The Australian Labor Party and the aid to parochial schools controversy. Univ Park, Pa, USA, Administrative Committee on Research, Pennsylvania State Univ, 1966. 55p.

(395) AUSTRALIA. Prime Minister's Department. The Commonwealth government in education. Canb, 1966. 56p.

(396) SANTAMARIA, B. A. State aid in perspective. Melb, Hawthorn Press, 1966. 24p.

1967 (397) FITZGERALD, R. T. Investment in education; a study of recent trends in expenditure. Hawthorn, Vic, ACER, 1967. 20p. (Quarterly Review of Australian Education, vol 1, no 1).

(398) MATHEWS, R. Meeting the crisis; federal aid for education. Melb, Victorian Fabian Society, 1967. 48p. (Victorian Fabian Society pamphlet 15).

1969 (399) DAVIS, R. P. State aid and Tasmanian politics, 1868-1920. Hobart, Univ of Tas, 1969. 135p.

(400) NEW South Wales Federation of Infants School Clubs. State aid; two words that spell controversy. Syd, 1969. 8p.

(401) VICTORIAN Teachers Union. A plan for action; federal aid for state schools. Melb, 1969. 12 leaves.

1970 (402) AUSTRALIAN Education Council. Nation wide survey of educational needs. Syd, Govt Pr, 1970. 14 leaves. Reprinted with an introduction by NSW Teachers Federation, Sydney, 1970.

(403) GAUSSEN, R. Taxation and education; a submission concerning increased taxation benefits for students and their parents. North Melb, NUAUS, 1970. 11p.

1971 (404) KITCHENN, R. G. State aid for non state schools. Melb, Aust Council of State School Organisations, 1971. 21p.

(405) NEW South Wales Teachers Federation. The myth of $460 million; an analysis of NSW State Government expenditure on education. [Syd, 1971?]. 11p.

1972 (406) PAPUA New Guinea. Manpower Planning Unit. Office of Programming and Co-ordination. Rates of return to investment in high level manpower in Papua New Guinea, 1970-71. Port Moresby, 1972. 39 leaves. (Manpower Studies, no 7).

2 Education in Practice (1)

Includes sections on (i) states and territories; (ii) preschool education;
(iii) primary education; (iv) secondary education; (v) technical education;
(vi) education for special groups: Australian Aborigines, adult education,
the handicapped, migrants, rural education.

(i) States and Territories

This section includes works that deal with systems of a single state.
Histories of state systems concerned mainly with the 19th century are
included in Section A2 (pages 12-14). Many of the general works in
this bibliography also include information about state systems. The
subject index must be used to obtain all references to a state system.

Australian Capital Territory

1967 (407) AUSTRALIAN National University, Canberra. Department of
      Adult Education. An independent education authority for the Austra-
      lian Capital Territory;report of a working party. Canb, 1967. 66p.

New South Wales

1924 (408) GOLLAN. K. The organisation and administration of education
      in New South Wales. Syd, Teachers College, [1924?] . 151p.

1935 (409) MACKENZIE, T. F. Nationalism and education in Australia,
      with special reference to NSW. Lond, P. S. King, 1935. 152p.

1946 (410) HEFFRON, R. J. Tomorrow is theirs; the present and
      future of education in New South Wales. Syd, Govt Pr, 1946. 135p.

      (411) LIBERAL Party of Australia. New South Wales Division.
      Research Section. Education in Australia. Syd, 1946. 20p.
      Contents: no 1. A survey of New South Wales. 8p.; no 2. The
      pre-school and infant-child. 12p.

      (412) NEW South Wales Public School Teachers Federation. A
      new deal for education demands large scale Commonwealth aid.
      Syd, 1946. 16p.

1948 (413) NEW South Wales. Department of Education. An outline of
      public education in New South Wales. Syd, Govt Pr, 1948.

1952 (414) HUNT, N. A new order in education before a new deal
      required. Narrandera, NSW, the Author, 1952. 7p.

1955 (415) BRAITHWAITE, J. M. and King, E. J. Multiple-class teaching; a study of the organisation and teaching practices of one-teacher schools in New South Wales, Australia. Paris, Educational Clearing House for Unesco, 1955. 42p. (Unesco Educational Studies and Documents, no 12).

1957 (416) CRANE, A. R. and Walker, W. G. Peter Board; his contribution to the development of education in New South Wales. Melb, ACER, 1957. 362p. (Educational Research Series, no 71).

1959 (417) NEW South Wales Teachers Federation. The case for an Education Commission: why and how. Syd, 1959. 31p.

1960 (418) NEW South Wales Teachers Federation. NSW public schools class loads and conditions, 1960. Syd, 1960. 26p.

1961 (419) NEW South Wales Teachers Federation. The problem of the schools; a survey of class-loads and conditions in NSW public schools during 1961. Syd, 1961. 39p.

1963 (420) RYAN, E. Parents guide to education in NSW. Syd, Horwitz-Grahame, 1963. 163p.

1965 (421) BARCAN, A. A short history of education in NSW. Syd, Martindale Press, 1965. 352p.

1969 (422) KENNETT, M. The teachers' challenge; professional standards and public service. Syd, Alpha Books, 1969. 159p.

(423) NEW South Wales. Department of Education. Division of Planning. Winds of change; administrative changes in education in New South Wales since 1953. Syd, Govt Pr. 1969. 6p.

1970 (424) FENLEY, W. J., editor. Education in the 1970s and 1980s; continuity and change in Australian education. 2nd ed. Syd, Hicks, Smith, 1970. 137p.
First published 1969 by the Department of Education, University of Sydney.

1971 (425) ENCEL, S. and Lepani, B. Education and planning in a new city; an opportunity for Campbelltown, NSW . Syd, Urban Systems Corporation, 1971. 27p.

1972 (426) NEW South Wales Teachers Federation. Three electorate survey. Syd, 1972. 28p.

(427) RAWLINSON, R. W. Overview, 1972 [of the Centre for Research in Learning and Instruction, Department of Education, NSW]. Syd, 1972. 1 vol (various pagination).

Papua and New Guinea

1936 (428) GROVES, W. C. Native education and culture-contact in New Guinea; a scientific approach. Melb, MUP, 1936. 179p. (ACER Education Research Series, no 46).

1951 (429) WILLIAMS, F. E. The blending of cultures: an essay on the aims of native education. Canb, Govt Pr, 1951. 45p. (Papua-New Guinea Department of Education Official Research Publication, no 1).

1958 (430) FRANK, D. Under the mango trees. Melb, OUP, 1958. 16p. (Stories of Our People Series). Reminiscences of a native teacher at Rogea, New Guinea.

1962 (431) PAPUA and New Guinea. Department of Native Affairs. Division of Development and Welfare. Welfare Section. Working with people; a guide for field officers of Papua and New Guinea. Port Moresby, 1962. 27p.

1963 (432) PAPUA and New Guinea. Department of Education. Teacher Training Division. Working with people; a manual for school supervisors and headmasters. Port Moresby, 1963. 20p.

1966 (433) VAN DER VEUR, K. and Richardson, P. Education through the eyes of an indigenous urban elite. Canb, New Guinea Research Unit, ANU, 1966. 102p.

1968 (434) ROE, E. Information, education and independence in Papua-New Guinea; inaugural lecture 1 August 1968. Boroko, TPNG, Univ of Papua and New Guinea, 1968. 22p.

1970 (435) PAPUA and New Guinea Institute of Technology Library. Education in Papua and New Guinea; a bibliography. Lae, TPNG, 1970. 19 leaves.

(436) PAPUA New Guinea. Department of Education. Opportunities for research in education and social development in the Territory of Papua and New Guinea. Konedobu, TPNG, 1970. 16p.

1971 (437) PAPUA New Guinea. Department of Education. Recent developments in education, 1971. [Konedobu, 1972]. 18p.

Queensland

1956 (438) QUEENSLAND. University. Progress report on resolutions of the 1955 conference with principals of secondary schools. St Lucia, Qld, 1956. 8p.

1963 (439) HANGER, T. Sixty years in Queensland schools. Syd, Wentworth Books, 1963. 110p.

1966 (440) BORCHART, F. T. The regional system of educational administration in the Wide Bay region, Queensland. Melb, ACER, 1966. 22p. (Information Bulletin, no 46).

1968 (441) GOODMAN, R. D. Secondary education in Queensland, 1860-1960. Canb, ANU Press, 1968. 405p.

1970 (442) QUEENSLAND. Department of Education. Education in Queensland. Brisb, 1970. 24p.

(443) QUEENSLAND Teachers Union. An education commission for Queensland. [Brisb,1970?]. 44p.

South Australia

1947 (444) SOUTH Australia. Department of Education. What our schools are doing. Adel, Govt Pr, 1947. 56p.
New edition published in 1970.

1967 (445) WISEMAN, R. Socio-economic status and academic success; a report to the South Australian Institute of Teachers Research Committee. Adel, SAIT, 1967. 27p.

1969 (446) HUMANIST Society of South Australia. Education Sub-Committee. Submission to Committee of Enquiry into Education in South Australia. Adel 1969. 26 leaves.

(447) ROPER, T. W. Submission to Committee of Enquiry into Education in South Australia. North Melb, NUAUS, 1969. 25 leaves.

(448) WISEMAN, R. A study of social class differences in performance and progress in a high school. Adel, SAIT, 1969. 27p.

1972 (449) SOUTH Australia. Education Department. Education 1992. Adel, 1972. 8p. (Primary Division Broadsheet, no 3).

Tasmania

1946 (450) TASMANIA. Education Department. Advance in education; 1886-1946, sixty years of progress in Tasmania, by B. W. Rait. Hobart, 1946. 23p.

Victoria

1908 (451) VICTORIA. Department of Education. Preliminary report of the Director of Education [Mr Frank Tate] made during an official visit to Europe and America; with recommendations referring to state education in Victoria. Melb, Govt Pr, 1908. 108p.

1913 (452) MURDOCH, W. L. F. The education problem in Victoria. Melb, Whitcombe & Tombs, [1913]. 40p.

1940 (453) VICTORIAN Teachers Union. Raising the school leaving age; an essential for the future of democracy. Melb, [194?]. 3p.

1942 (454) HENDERSON, N. K. What chance has your child? Melb, Research Group of the Left Book Club of Vic, 1942. 76p.
'A study of educational opportunity in Victoria' (subtitle on cover).

1944 (455) TOWARD better education: a plea for reform: being the reprinting of a series of articles originally published in the Argus, Melbourne. Melb, Argus and Australasian, 1944. 16p.

1945 (456) VICTORIA. Council of Public Education. Report on educational reform and development in Victoria. Melb, 1945. 42p.

1954 (457) RETURNED Sailors, Soldiers and Airmen's Imperial League
of Australia. Victorian Branch. Victorian educational facilities
and particulars of scholarships available 1954/55. 2nd ed. Melb,
1954. 67p.

1956 (458) ANCHEN, J.O. Frank Tate and his work for education.
Melb, ACER, 1956. 236p. (Educational Research Series, no 69).

1957 (459) VICTORIA. Education Department. Information Service.
Notes on the Victorian education system (1-7-55). Melb, 1957.
12 leaves.

1964 (460) AUSTRALIAN Labor Party. Victorian Branch. Looking
to the future; Labor's plan for education in Victoria. Melb, 1964.
59p.

1966 (461) AUSTRALIAN Labor Party. Victorian Branch. Looking to
the future; a plan for education in Victoria. Melb, 1966. 104p.

(462) DOW, G. M. and others. Parent, pupil and school; Victoria's
education system. Melb, Cassell, 1966. 222p.

(463) VICTORIAN Teachers Union. A child deprived; a report
from the teachers in technical schools to the people of Victoria.
[Melb, 1966]. 8p.

1968 (464) O'NEILL, J. and Paterson, J. The cost of free education;
schools and low income families. Melb, Cheshire, 1968. 82p.
A research study of the Brotherhood of St Laurence

1969 (465) THOMPSON, L. H. S. Looking ahead in education. Melb,
Education Dept, 1969. 98p.
Written by the Minister of Education, Victoria.

1970 (466) LAWRY, J. R. and Bessant, B. Oral history archives re-
search project, 1968-69; index. Melb, Monash Univ Faculty of
Education, 1970. 30p.
An index of taped interviews held by Monash University.

1971 (467) VICTORIA. Education Department. Education '71. Melb,
1971. 8p.

1972 (468) ROPER, T. W. [Education in the western suburbs: paper
presented at] 72 Seminar The Deprived West, Sunshine, May 7
1972. [Melb, 1972]. 17 leaves.

Western Australia

1943 (469) STATE School Teachers Union of Western Australia. Education in Western Australia; proposals for immediate reconstruction.
Perth, 1943. 11p.

(ii) Preschool Education

1932 (470) GUTTERIDGE, M. V. The story of an Australian nursery
school. Melb, MUP, 1932. 31p.
The school is Keele Street Free Kindergarten, Collingwood, Vic.

1944 (471) BENJAMIN, Z. Education for parenthood. Melb, ACER,
1944. 48p. (Future of Education Series, no 7).

(472) CUMPSON, J. H. L. and Heinig, C. M. Preschool centres in
Australia; building, equipment and programme. Canb, Dept of
Health, 1944. 240p.

1946 (473) COUGHLAN, W. G. Nursery schools; blessing, or - ?
Syd, Christian Social Order Movement, 1946. 8p.

1947 (474) FREE Kindergarten Union of Victoria. Prelude to school;
a series of articles dealing with the welfare of children, especially
of preschool age. Compiled by the Free Kindergarten Union of
Victoria, the Nursery Kindergarten Extension Board and the
Kindergarten Training College. Melb, 1947. 64p.

1958 (475) ROBERTS, M. J. Planning the programme in a preschool
centre. Canb, Australian Preschool Assn, 1958. 24p.
Second edition 1964.

1962 (476) AUSTRALIAN Preschool Association Conference, 9th,
University of Tasmania, 1961. Unity and continuity in the education of young children. Melb, [1962]. 115p.

1964 (477) LINDBERG, L. Report concerning visits to preschool in
Australia centres. Canb, Publications Subcommittee, Australian
Preschool Assn, 1964. Folder (6p).

1967 (478) NATIONAL Library of Austral ia. The preschool child;
a list of Australian works. Canb, 1967. 24p.

(479) WALKER, M. and others. Teaching in the preschool kindergarten. Syd, Novak, 1967. 175p.

1968 (480) FITZGERALD, R. T. and de Lemos, M. M. Current trends
in preschool education. Hawthorn, Vic, ACER, 1968. 30p.
(Quarterly Review of Australian Education, vol 1 no 4).
Contents: Facilities in preschooling in Australia by R. T. Fitzgerald;
Some recent developments; theory and practice by M. M. de Lemos.
Supplement (p 33-41) contains comments.

(481) RIDLEY, J. I. Starting school; an infant teacher talks to
parents. Blackburn, Vic, Acacia Press, [1968?]. 29p.

1969 (482) AUSTRALIAN Preschool Association. Conference, 12th,
University of Adelaide, 1969. Children in a changing world:
[papers]. Canb, Australian Preschool Assn, 1969. 151p.

1970 (483) AUSTRALIA. Department of Labour and National Service.
Women's Bureau. Child care centres. Melb, 1970. 68p. (Women
in the Work Force Series Booklet, no 7).

(484) AUSTRALIAN Preschool Association. Victorian Branch.
The preschool field in Victoria; report of a subcommittee. Melb,
1970. 25p.

(485) BRAGGETT, E. J., editor. Preschool education; proceedings of a Conference on Preschool Education held at the University
of Newcastle, November 1970. Newcastle, Univ of Newcastle
Dept of Education, 1970. 62p.

(486) QUEENSLAND. Department of Education. Van Leer
Foundation Project. Research report on some aspects of the
language development of preschool children. Brisb.,1970. 101p.

1971 (487) AUSTRALIAN Preschool Association. New South Wales
Branch. Seminar, 2 May 1970; papers presented by A. Fountain
and G. Masselos. [Syd, 1971?]. 22p.

(488) DE LEMOS, M. M. Controversy in preschool education.
Hawthorn, Vic, ACER, 1971. 45p. (Occasional Paper no 4).

(489) FITZGERALD, R. T. and Crosher, J. A. Preschool education
in Australia; a review of recent developments. Hawthorn, Vic,
ACER, 1971. 38p. (Occasional Paper no 5).

(490) WATERS, J. Helping in kindergarten. Melb, Australian
Preschool Assn, 1971. 16p.

1972 (491) ASHBY, G. F. Preschool theories and strategies. Carlton,
Vic, MUP, 1972. 79p. (Second Century in Australian Education,
no 6).

(iii) Primary Education

1914 (492) TASMANIA. Education Department. History of the development of the curriculum of state primary schools in Tasmania.
Hobart, Govt Pr, 1914. 17p. (Educational Monograph, no 1).

1924 (493) ELIJAH, J. W. and Cole, J. A. The principles and techniques
of teaching in elementary schools. Melb, Whitcombe & Tombs,
1924.
2nd edition, no date; 3rd edition, 1944; 4th edition, 1962 written
by Cole, J. A. and Blake, L. J. (see entry 504, page 45).

1932 (494) COLE, P. R., editor. The primary school curriculum in
Australia. Melb, MUP, 1932. 324p. (ACER Educational Research
Series, no 16).

(495) WYNDHAM, H. S. Class grouping in the primary school; a
study of the nature and validity of current methods of class grouping
in Sydney primary schools. Melb, MUP, 1932. 139p. (ACER
Educational Research Series, no 9).

1935 (496) REEVES, C. A history of Tasmanian education; state
primary education. Melb, MUP, 1935. 141p. (ACER Educational
Research Series, no 40).

1943 (497) BRAITHWAITE, J. M., McRae, C. R. and Staines, R. G.
Reform in the primary school. Melb, ACER, 1943. 40p.
(Future of Education Series, no 4).

1952 (498) AUSTRALIAN Council for Educational Research. Primary
school studies. Melb, 1952.
Nine issues were published: 1. The approach to reading; 2. The
individual child; 3. Ends and means in arithmetic; 4. The appraisal
of results; 5. Highway of expression; 6. The purposes of teaching;
7. Power over words; 8. Children in groups; 9. Priorities in the
primary school.

1955 (499) BLAKEMORE, G. L. Individualising education in the elementary school. Wagga Wagga, NSW Daily Advertiser, 1955.
95p.

1957 (500) AUSTRALIAN Council for Educational Research. Admission
to school and promotion in infants grades; a descriptive account
of Australian educational policies and practices. Melb, 1957. 61
leaves.

(501) AUSTRALIAN Council for Educational Research. The early
years; a summary of an enquiry into age of admission, classification and promotion practices in Australian primary schools.
Melb, 1957. 16p.

1958 (502) PRIMARY education today: five lectures at a series arranged
by the Victorian Institute of Educational Research, 1958, edited by
D. H. Price. Melb, VIER, 1960. 72p.
Contents: Changing concepts of primary education by H. P.
Schoenheimer; Teachers, children and parents by L. Hooper;
The teaching of arithmetic by J. A. Cole; The teaching of reading
by D. C. Streader; The significance of modern art education by
M. C. Dimmack.

1961 (503) BALL, D. G., Cunningham, K. S. and Radford, W. C.
Supervision and inspection of primary schools. Melb, ACER,
1961. 269p. (Research Series, no 73).

1962 (504) COLE, J. A. and Blake, L. J. Principles and techniques of
teaching. Melb, Whitcombe & Tombs, 1962. 460p.
Fourth edition of 'The principles and techniques of teaching in
elementary schools' by J. W. Elijah and J. A. Cole (entry 493,
page 44).

1963 (505) QUEENSLAND. Department of Education. Research and
Guidance Branch. Standards of achievement in the basic subjects,
Queensland Grade 7 pupils. Brisb, 1963. 19 leaves. (Bulletin
no 25).

1964 (506) BASSETT, G. W. Each one is different; teaching for individual differences in the primary school; a contribution to the individual education of Australian children, arising from a conference
convened by ACER in August 1962. Melb, ACER, 1964. 153p.
Revised edition published in 1968.

(507) SOUTH Australian Institute of Teachers. Children over 14 years in South Australian primary schools. Adel, 1964. 10p.

1966 (508) JONES, O. R. The primary school. Melb, Cheshire, 1966. 165p.

1967 (509) BASSETT, G. W., editor. Teaching in the primary school. Syd, Novak, 1967. 343p.

1969 (510) WARRY, R. S. and Fitzgerald, R. T. The new Rs in the Australian primary school. Hawthorn, Vic, ACER, 1969. 25p. (Quarterly Review of Australian Education, vol 2, no 4).

1970 (511) SEMINAR for Primary Principals, Somers Camp, 1970. Policy making; [seminar report]. Melb, Education Dept, 1970. 1 vol (various pagination).

(512) VICTORIA. Education Department. The primary school. Melb, 1970. 27p.

(513) WESTERN Australia. Education Department. Inservice education 1970, primary: involvement in change. Perth, 1970. 85p.

1971 (514) CREATIVITY: [papers from a] seminar for principals of the Mildura Inspectorate [on] primary school administration, June 1971. [Mildura, Vic, 1971?].1 vol (various pagination).

(515) SEMINAR for Primary Principals, Somers Camp, 1971. Change and the principal; seminar report. Melb, Education Dept, 1971. 81p.

(iv) Secondary Education

1930 (516) MELBOURNE. University. Professorial Board. Secondary school education in Victoria; report on the A and B class system of the University of Melbourne, by T. M. Cherry. Melb, MUP, 1930. 11p.

1935 (517) COLE, P. R., editor. The education of the adolescent in Australia; [report of a committee]. Melb, MUP, 1935. 364p. (ACER Educational Research Series, no 32).
Papers contributed by P. Board; F. Tate; H. T. Lovell; A. Mackie; J. A. Seitz; R. G. Cameron; K. S. Cunningham; H. L. Harris; C. E. Fletcher; J. R. Darling.

(518) ELLIOTT, W. J. Secondary education in New South Wales. Melb, MUP, 1935. 42p. (ACER Educational Research Series, no 38).

1945 (519) STATE School Teachers Union of Western Australia. Secondary education for today and tomorrow in Western Australia. Perth, the Union, 1945. 8p.

1950 (520) SCHONELL, F. J. Modern developments in secondary education in England with special reference to Queensland. Brisb, Queensland Inst for Educational Research, 1950. 23p.

1955 (521) QUEENSLAND. University. A report of the conference
between university staff and Queensland secondary school principals,
5 and 6 May 1955 at the University of Queensland, St Lucia,
Brisbane, Queensland. St Lucia, Qld, 1955. 96p.

1960 (522) AUSTRALIAN Institute of Political Science. Spring forum,
Sydney, September 10-22 1960. Secondary education; the Wyndham
report: a set of three lectures. Syd, 1960. 47p.
Contents: The need for change by H. S. Wyndham; Changing the
organisation of secondary education by T. Miller; The community
and changes in secondary education by F. S. Bradhurst.

1961 (523) CONNELL, W. F. The foundations of secondary education.
Melb, ACER, 1961. 137p. (Monographs on Secondary Education,
no 1).
Revised edition, 1967.

(524) NEW England University. Department of Adult Education.
Secondary education in New South Wales; lectures and discussions
on the Wyndham report. Armidale, 1961. 127p.

(525) PRICE, D. H. , editor. Secondary education today; four
lectures given at a series arranged by the Victorian Institute of
Educational Research, 1959. Melb, The Institue, 1961. 47p.
Contents: The tasks of the secondary school by T. H. Coates;
The organisation of secondary education by A. McDonell; Eval-
uation and testing in the secondary school by G. D. Bradshaw;
School counselling by R. R. Priestley.

1962 (526) QUEENSLAND. Department of Education. Research and
Guidance Branch. An evaluation of the modified course in five
Brisbane High Schools, 1961. Brisb, 1962. 17 leaves. (Bulletin
no 23).

(527) RADFORD, W. C. A prediction of secondary school enrolments
and of potential university enrolments in Australia. Melb, ACER,
1962. 31p.

1964 (528) NEAL, W. D. The secondary school curriculum; a review of
developments in Western Australia, 1958-64, with proposals for
the future. Perth, Education Dept, 1964. 62p.

1965 (529) DRINKWATER, D. J. Developments in early adolescence and
the structure of secondary education; an interstate survey. St
Lucia, Qld Univ Press, 1965. 51p. (University of Queensland
Papers, Faculty of Education, vol 1, no 5).

1966 (530) NEW South Wales. Secondary Schools Board. The first
four years; secondary education in New South Wales, forms 1-1V.
Syd, 1966. 16p.

(531) VICTORIAN Secondary Teachers Association. Staffing crisis
in Victorian State Secondary Schools, March 1966; a preliminary
report on a survey conducted by the ... Association between Monday
7 March 1966 and Friday 11 March 1966. Melb, 1966. 6p.

1967 (532) FITZGERALD, R. T. The new secondary school population
in Australia; trends in student retention. Hawthorn, Vic, ACER,
1967. 18p. (Quarterly Review of Australian Education, vol 1 no 2).

1968 (533) FITZGERALD, R. T. Secondary schools in the sixties;
framework and organisation. Hawthorn, Vic, ACER, 1968. 20p.
(Quarterly Review of Australian Education, vol 1 no 3).

1970 (534) AUSTRALIAN Frontier. Consultation on secondary education
in a changing society. Malvern, Vic, 1970. 36p.

(535) FITZGERALD, R. T. The secondary school at sixes and
sevens; a review of the sixties and prospect of the seventies.
Hawthorn, Vic, ACER, 1970. 252p.

(536) HANNAFORD, B. D. A report on the South Australian
secondary school in the seventies. Adel, South Australian Institute
of Teachers, 1970 . 47p.

(537) QUEENSLAND. Department of Education. Queensland state
schools; the secondary scene. Brisb, 1970. 20p.

(538) SOUTH Australia. Education Department. Our secondary
schools. Adel, 1970. 32p.

1971 (539) AUSTRALIAN College of Education. ACT Chapter. Seminar
on junior colleges, Canberra, March 1971; summary of papers
presented. Canb, Dept of Education and Science, 1971. 25p.

(v) Technical Education

1909 (540) NEW South Wales. Department of Technical Education.
A quarter-century of technical education in New South Wales.
Syd, Govt Pr, 1909. 331p.

1930 (541) FENNER, C. and Paull, A. G. Individual education; being
an account of an experiment in operation at the Thebarton Technical
High School, South Australia. Melb, MUP, 1930. 40p. (ACER
Educational Research Series, no 1).
Paper read before the Education Section of the Australasian Assoc-
iation for the Advancement of Science, Brisbane 1930.

1934 (542) VICTORIAN Technical Schools Exhibition, Melbourne 1934.
Technical education in Victoria, 1868-1934. Melb, Melb Technical
College, 1934. 32p.

1936 (543) DRUMMOND, D. H. Technical education in Australia;
administration and finance. Syd, Govt Pr, 1936. 16p.

(544) SUBLET, F. G. Education for industry and citizenship.
Melb, MUP, 1936. 143p. (ACER Educational Research Series
no 45).

1943 (545) ELTHAM, E. P. Technical education in war and peace, an
address delivered to members of the Institute of Industrial Management on 6 April 1943. Melb, Vic Chamber of Manufacturers, 1943.
32p.

1945 (546) ELLIS, F. Education for industry. Melb, Vic Chamber of Manufacturers, 1945. 35p.

(547) ELTHAM, E. P. Educational rehabilitation of men and women of the services with particular reference to technical and vocational training. Melb, Dept of Labour and National Service, 1945. 20p. Address delivered to the Peoples Educational Conference, Canberra on 25 April 1945.

1946 (548) PHILLIPS, L. W. and Cunningham, K. S. Education for livelihood. Melb, ACER, 1946. 49p. (Future of Education Series, no 10).

1947 (549) ROYAL Australian Air Force. Vocational guidance in the RAAF, 1942-46. Melb, 1947. 80p.

1953 (550) QUEENSLAND. Department of Public Instruction. Research and Guidance Branch. Investigations of clerical and shorthand aptitude. Brisb, 1953. 34 leaves. (Bulletin no 8).

1957 (551) COPLAND, D. B. Administrative staff training: a new frontier in education. Melb, Cheshire, 1957. 26p. (Australian Administrative Staff College Papers, no 1).
Fourth Frank Tate Memorial Lecture, 1957.

(552) QUEENSLAND. Department of Public Instruction. Research and Guidance Branch. Predicting success in electrical apprenticeship courses. Brisb, 1957. 18 leaves. (Bulletin no 14).

1958 (553) NEW South Wales. Department of Technical Education. Seventy five years of technical education, 1883-1958. Syd, Govt Pr, 1958. 3 vols.

(554) RADFORD, W. C. Some characteristics of students proceeding to higher technical education. Melb, ACER, 1958. 5 leaves. (Information Bulletin, no 36).

1964 (555) FITZGERALD, R. T. Current trends in vocational and technical training in Australia. Melb, ACER, 1964. 10p.
Report prepared for the Director General of Higher Technical Education, Ministry of Labour, Madrid, Spain.

(556) WILLIAMS, H. S. Technical education in Australia; collected papers. Perth, Technical Publications Trust, 1964. 88p.

1965 (557) WALTER, M. R. Report to the acting principal on the numbers, entrance standards and performance of overseas students in technical institutions in Australia, with particular reference to Victoria. Melb, Royal Melb Inst of Technology Press, 1965. 74p.

1966 (558) AUSTRALIA. Department of Labour and National Service. Outline of vocational training in Australia. Canb, 1966. 39p. Similar outlines also prepared in 1966 for Ceylon, India, Indonesia; Japan, Kenya, Korea, Malawi, Malaysia, New Zealand, Pakistan, Singapore, Tanzania, Thailand, the Philipines, Zambia, for the Pan Indian Ocean Conference on Technical Education and Training, Perth, 1966.

(559) AUSTRALIAN Apprenticeship Advisory Committee. Essential features of Australian apprenticeship systems. Melb, Dept of Labour and National Service, 1966. 1 vol (various pagination).

1967 (560) AUSTRALIAN Council of Employers Federations. Training the future work force; some aspects of needs and responsibilities. [Melb, 1967?]. 8p.

1968 (561) DUNCANSON, W. E. Technical education in Papua and New Guinea. Melb, Papua New Guinea Society of Vic, 1968. 13 leaves.

1969 (562) FARGHER, F. T. The first twenty five years; being a short history of the Association of Principals of Victorian Technical Institutions, 1939-66. Melb, Melb School of Printing & Graphic Arts, 1969. 53p.

(563) QUEENSLAND. Committee of Apprenticeship Examiners. Examining in the technical college. Brisb, 1969. 20p.

1970 (564) TECHNICAL education and industrial training; proceedings of the Lae seminar, 9-11 October 1969. Konedobu, TPNG, Technical Education Consultative Committee, 1970. 264p.

(565) WORLD Confederation of Organisations of the Teaching Profession. Technical and vocational seminar, Sydney 1970: [papers and discussions]. Brisb, W. Brooks, 1970. 33p. (A special publication of the Technical Teachers Association of Australia).

1971 (566) NEW South Wales. Department of Technical Education. Survey of needs of technical education in New South Wales, 1971-75. Syd, 1971. 50p.

(vi) Education for Special Groups

(a) Australian Aborigines

1935 (567) BENNETT, M. M. Teaching the aborigines: data from Mount Margaret Mission, WA, 1935. Perth, United Aborigines Mission, 1935. 67p.

1936 (568) SCHENK, R. S. The educability of the native. Perth, Mount Margaret Mission, 1936. 46p.

1937 (569) KEESING, F. M. Education in Pacific countries: interpreting a seminar. Conference of educators and social scientists ... Hawaii, 1936. Shanghai, Kelly & Walsh, 1937. 234p.
Aim of the conference was 'to study for 5 weeks the common problems of education and cultural adjustment among peoples living within the Pacific Ocean area. '

1948 (570) BECKENHAM, P. W. The education of the Australian aborigine. Melb, ACER, 1948. 55p.

1960 (571) SCHONELL, F. J. , Meddleton, I. G. and Watts, B. H.
School attainment and home backgrounds of aboriginal children
in Queensland. Brisb, Univ of Qld Press, 1960. 44p. (University
of Queensland Paper, vol 1 no 3. Faculty of Education Research
Study, no 7, 1960).

1964 (572) ASSOCIATION for the Assimilation of Aborigines, Armidale,
NSW. Aborigines Welfare Board bursaries. Armidale, NSW, 1964.
10p.

(573) GUNTON, E. J. , compiler. Education of Australiañ aborigines.
Adel, Public Library of SA, 1964. 10p. (South Australia Public
Library. Research Service. Bibliographies, Series 4, no 27).

(574) NEW South Wales Teachers Federation. A survey of aboriginal children iñ NSW schools. Syd, 1964. 8p. Further survey, 1968.

1965 (575) PENNY, H. H. Tribal aborigines, an educated people;
some thoughts on the meaning of education for aborigines and
other Australians. Adel, Aborigines Advancement League Inc,
SA, 1965. 7p.

1966 (576) CONSULTATIVE Committee on Aboriginal Education. Sub-
missions to the Joint Committee of the Legislative Council and
Legislative Assembly upon aborigines' welfare, March 1966.
[Syd, Univ of Syd?], 1966. 48p.

(577) DUNCAN, A. T. Aboriginal education: are the problems
inique? Syd, Dept of Adult Education, Univ of Syd, 1966. 8p.
Paper presented at a Conference on aboriginal education organised
by the Department of Adult Education, University of Sydney and
the Consultative Committee on Aboriginal Education.

1969 (578) DUNN, S. S. and Tatz, C. M. , editors. Aborigines and
education. Melb, Sun Books in association with Centre for Research
into Aboriginal Affairs, Monash University, 1969. 347p.

(579) ROPER, T. W. , editor. Aboriginal education; the teacher's
role. North Melb, Abschol, NUAUS, 1969. 236p.
Papers presented at a Summer School on Aboriginal Education
and the Teacher's Role held in Sydney in January 1968.

1970 (580) NEW South Wales Teachers Federation. Aboriginal children
at school; special problems and special needs. Syd, 1970. 24p.

(581) QUEENSLAND. Department of Education. Van Leer Project.
Research report on some aspects of the language development of
preschool children. Brisb, 1970. 101p.

1971 (582) AUSTRALIAN College of Education. ACT Chapter. The
education of aborigines; papers from a seminar, 25 September
1971. Canb, 1971. 23p.

(583) BRUCE, D. W., Hengeveld, M. and Radford, W. C. Some
cognitive skills in aboriginal children in Victorian primary schools.
Hawthorn, Vic, ACER, 1971. 32p. (Progress Report, no 2).

(584) McDONALD, C. Survey of aboriginal children in NSW
secondary schools. Syd, NSW Teachers Federation, 1971.
7 leaves.

(585) TATZ, C. M. Themes for a change. North Melb, Aboriginal
Scholarships Society, 1971. 21p.

1972 (586) McMAHON, W. Australian aborigines; Commonwealth policy
and achievements. Canberra, [Aust Govt Publishing Service],
1972. 15p.

(587) NATIONAL Workshop on Aboriginal Education, Brisbane
1971. Report; priorities for action and research, edited by B. H.
Watts. St Lucia, Department of Education, University of Queensland, 1972. 257p.

(b) Adult Education

1939 (588) WILMOT, R. W. E. The Melbourne Athenaeum, 1839-1939;
history and records of the institution. Melb, The Athenaeum, 1939.
64p.

1941 (589) CENTRAL Cultural Council. Culture in war time: being
proceedings of a conference held on 1 September 1940. Syd, 1941.
45p.

1944 (590) BADGER, C. R. Adult education in post-war Australia.
Melb, ACER, 1944. 32p. (Future of Education, no 8).

(591) DUNCAN, W. G. K. , editor. The future of adult education in
Australia: address and papers given ... at a conference organised
by the Workers Educational Association of NSW. Syd, WEA (NSW),
1944. 72p.

1947 (592) BADGER, C. R. Maecenas or Moloch; the state and adult
education. Melb, Cheshire, 1947. 20p. (John Smyth Memorial
Lecture, 1947).

(593) COUNCIL of Adult Education of Victoria. A speech at the
first meeting of the Council ... by Mr. Francis Field ... May 23rd
1947. 12p. (Pamphlet no 1).

1948 (594) SHORT summer courses in England arranged by the British
Council. Melb, ACER, 1948. 9 leaves. Information Bulletin,
no 12).
1949 edition. (Information Bulletin, no 16).
1950 edition. (Information Bulletin, no 19).

1949 (595) HUNTER, P. E. The Brisbane School of Arts Centenary,
1849-1949. Brisb, Brisbane School of Arts, 1949. 44p.

1951 (596) PEERS, R. Adult education in Australia: a report. [Canb,
COE, 1951?]. 25p.

1959 (597) ALEXANDER, F. Adult education in Australia; an historian's
point of view. Melb, Cheshire, 1959. 44p.

1960 (598) SHEATS, P. H. A report on university adult education in Australia and New Zealand. Chicago, Centre for the study of Liberal Education for Adults, 1960. 53p. (Notes and Essays on Education for Adults, no 27).

1962 (599) PAPUA and New Guinea. Department of Native Affiars. Division of Development and Welfare. Welfare Section. Working with people; a guide for field officers of Papua and New Guinea. Port Moresby, 1962. 27p.

1963 (600) SYDNEY University. Department of Tutorial Classes. Kits; a new way of learning through group activities. Syd, [1963?]. 16p.

1964 (601) UNESCO Regional Seminar on the Role of Schools and Universities in Adult Education, Sydney, 1964. Report. Syd, Australian National Advisory Committee for Unesco, 1964. 128p.

1965 (602) COUNCIL of Adult Education, Victoria. Learning for living, today and tomorrow; proceedings of a one day seminar held at the Adult Education Centre, Melbourne, 14 August 1965. Melb, Council of Adult Education and Adult Education Assn of Vic, 1965. 31p.

(603) CREW, V. A bibliography of adult education, 1835-1965. Canb, National Library of Aust in association with the Aust Assn of Adult Education, 1968. 107p.

1968 (604) AUSTRALIAN Association of Adult Education. Conference, 8th, University of New England, Armidale, NSW 1968. Adult education, the next ten years; proceedings. Armidale, NSW, 1968. 1 vol (various pagination).

1969 (605) CROWLEY, D. W., editor. The role of colleges of advanced education in Australian adult education, Syd, Aust Assn of Adult Education, 1969. 54p. (Australian Association of Adult Education, Monograph no 1).
Papers arising from Syndicate Discussions at the National Conference on Adult Education arranged by the Australian Association of Adult Education at the University of New England, Armidale, August 1968.

(606) DURSTON, B. H., editor. Planning and organising programmes in adult education. Armidale, NSW, Department of Education, University of New England, 1969. 39p. (New England Papers on Education, no 3).

(607) WHITELOCK, D., editor. Adult education in Australia. Rushcutters Bay, NSW, Pergamon Press Aust, 1970. 295p. 'The first in the field, a spectrum of opinion reflecting as many aspects of work as possible' (editor's note).

1971 (608) HAINES, N. Continuing education and responsible society; a study of some principles of policy. Canb, Aust Assn of Adult Education, 1971. 84p. (Australian Association of Adult Education Monograph, no 2).

(609) WESSON, A., editor. Basic readings in Australian adult education. Melb, Council of Adult Education, 1971. 142p.

1972 (610) GANNICOTT, K. Recurrent education; a preliminary cost - benefit analysis. Hawthorn, Vic, ACER, 1972. 24p. (Occasional Paper no 6).

(c) Handicapped

1932 (611) PARKER, H. T. Intelligence and scholastic attainment; a study of the educational proficiency of subnormal children. Melb, MUP, 1932. 64p. (ACER Educational Research Series, no 17).

1934 (612) BACHELARD, P. M. The education of the retarded child. Melb, MUP, 1934. 92p. (ACER Educational Research Series, no 26).

(613) PARKER, H. T. The development of intelligence in subnormal children. Melb, MUP, 1934. 63p. (ACER Educational Research Series, no 27).

1937 (614) HILL, T. B. The classification and education of mentally handicapped children in various countries, by T. B. Hill; edited by D. J. A. Verco. Melb, MUP, 1937. 104p. (ACER Educational Research Series, no 47).

1940 (615) PHILLIPS, G. E. The constancy of the intelligence quotient in subnormal children. Melb, MUP, 1940. 86p. (ACER Educational Research Series, no 60).

1942 (616) SCHONELL, Sir F. J. Backwardness in the basic subjects. Edinb, Oliver and Boyd, 1942. 560p.

1949 (617) PARKER, H. T. The mental defective in school and after. Melb, MUP for ACER, 1949. 31p.

1950 (618) VICTORIA. Education Department. Visit of Dr and Mrs Ewing, August 1950. Melb, 1950. 13 leaves.

1958 (619) SCHONELL, F. J., Richardson, J. A. and McConnell, T. S. The subnormal child at home. Lond, Macmillan for Aust Council of Organisations for Subnormal Children, 1958. 173p.

1959 (620) SCHONELL, F. J., Meddleton, I. G., Watts, B. H. and Rorke, M. W. First and second surveys of the effects of a subnormal child on the family unit. Brisb, Qld Univ Press, 1959. 24p. (University of Queensland Papers, Faculty of Education vol 1, no 2).

1961 (621) AUSTRALIAN Council for the Mentally Retarded. Conference, 9th, Sydney, 1961. Recent developments in the field of mental retardation; record of a conference. Syd, 1961. 35p.

(622) SOUTH Australian Oral School Inc. Introducing opportunity for the deaf child to hear and speak. Adel, 1961. 13p.

1962 (623) SCHONELL, F. J. , McLeod, J. and Cochrane, R. G. , editors.
The slow learner; segregation or integration. Brisb, Qld Univ
Press, 1962. 99p.

1963 (624) NEALE, M. D. and Campbell, W. J. Education for the
intellectually limited child and adolescent. Syd, Novak, 1963.
167p.

1964 (625) BURCHETT, J. H. Utmost for the highest; the story of the
Victorian School for Deaf Children. Melb, Hall's Book Store
[for the Vic School for Deaf Children], 1964. 256p.

1967 (626) BRERETON, B. le Gay and Sattler, J. Cerebal palsy, basic
abilities; a plan for training the preschool child. Mosman, NSW,
Spastic Centre of NSW, 1967. 178p.

(627) TASMANIA. Education Department. Educational facilities
in Tasmania for handicapped children. [Hobart, Govt Pr, 1967?] .
24p.

1968 (628) ELDRIDGE, M. A history of the treatment of speech disorders.
Melb, Cheshire, 1968. 340p.

(629) McLEOD, J. , editor. The slow learner in the primary school.
Syd, Novak, 1968. 198p.

(630) PENGILLEY, P. By word of mouth; a rehabilitation course
in better hearing, lip reading and speech conversation, Australian
triple approach. Melb, Aust Assn for Better Hearing, 1968. 97p.

(631) QUEENSLAND. Department of Education. Research and
Curriculum Branch. The physical, behavioural and learning
patterns of rubella-affected children: report no 1. Brisb, 1968.
59p. (Bulletin no 35).

(632) QUEENSLAND. Department of Education. Research and
Curriculum Branch. Psycholinguistic research in Queensland
schools, 1961-66. Prepared in collaboration with N. W. M. Hart.
Brisb, 1968. 92p. (Bulletin no 34).

(633) VAN PELT, J. D. Parent groups for the mentally retarded
in America; a report on the organisation and functioning of the
National Association for Retarded Children at national, state and
local levels. Canb, the Author, 1968. 26p.
Prepared under a 1967 Rosemary A. Dybwad Grant.

1969 (634) AUTISTIC Childrens Association of South Australia. Autism;
cure tomorrow, care today. Proceedings of a conference on the
autistic child held at Adelaide, South Australia 16-18 August 1967.
Warradale, SA, [1969?] . 124p.

(635) CENTRE industries; adult training unit of the Spastic Centre
of New South Wales [papers] presented to Eleventh World Congress
International Society for Rehabilitation of the Disabled, Dublin,
1969. Syd, Spastic Centre of NSW, 1969. 40p.

(636) CONFERENCE of Sheltered Workshop Managers, Sydney, 1968. Report. Syd, Aust Council for Rehabilitation of Disabled, [1969?]. 77p.

(637) ROYAL New South Wales Institution for Deaf and Blind Children. Specialised residential school for children who are both deaf and blind, proposed national scheme; submission. [Syd? 1969?]. 1 vol (unpaged).

1970 (638) AUSTRALIAN College of Education. Subnormal children; report to NSW Chapter of the Australian College of Education. [Syd?], 1970. 39p.

(639) CLEMENTS, S. D. [Children with specific learning disabilities]: a public lecture, March 1970. Melb, Specific Learning Difficulties Assn of Vic, [1970?]. 24p.

(640) CLEMENTS, S. D. [Early identification, the multi-disciplinary diagnosis, and the educational management of children with learning disabilities]: a lecture for teachers and discussion with university staff, March 1970. Melb, Specific Learning Difficulties Assn of Vic, [1970?]. 53p.

(641) EPSTEIN, J. Image of the king: a parent's story of mentally handicapped children. Syd, Ure Smith, 1970. 142p.

(642) JOHN, N. S. Address to the Australian Association of Teachers of the Deaf (Victorian Branch) 7 October 1970. Annesley, Qld, Aust Assn of Teachers of the Deaf, 1970. 6 leaves.

(643) NEW South Wales. Inter-Departmental Committee on the Intellectually Handicapped. Intellectually handicapped; a bibliography of material in the libraries of the New South Wales Departments of Child Welfare and Social Welfare, Education, and Public Health. Syd, Govt Pr, 1970. 35p.

1971 (644) ANDERSON, J., editor. Learning disabilities; diagnosis and treatment. Armidale, NSW, Univ of New England, 1971. 132p.
Proceedings of a seminar held at the University of New England, February 1971.

(645) AUSTRALIAN College of Education. Some aspects of the education of handicapped children in Australia. Melb, 1971. 75p.
Contents: Subnormal children by NSW Chapter Sub-Committee; The reorganisation of educational facilities in Australia for children with speech and/or hearing impairments by P. Gorman; Classroom organisation, planning and procedures for the effective education of children with specific learning disabilities by J. M. Hills.

(646) AUSTRALIAN Frontier. Consultation on educational research for the mentally handicapped. Malvern, Vic, 1971. 35p.
Papers by L. C. Higgins on Research into the education of the mentally handicapped; and K. E. Johnson on The refining of educational diagnosis and its application to the specific learning needs of the intellectually handicapped.

(647) COCHRANE, K. J. , editor. The child with learning problems; a multi-disciplinary symposium. Brisb, Fred and Eleanor Schonell Educational Research Centre, Univ of Qld, 1971. 37p.
Papers by H. Connell, D. Fraser, M. Outridge, E. Chamberlain, N. Slorach, M. Ticehurst and W. C. Apelt.

(648) CORDWELL, A. M. Out of the silence; a book for the families and friends of hearing handicapped children. Syd, Alella Books, 1971. 135p.

(649) HUNDLEY, J. M. The small outsider; the story of an autistic child. Syd, A & R, 1971. 150p.

(650) NIEDER-HEITMAN, N. A survey of the modern history of deaf education. Stanmore, NSW, Adult Deaf and Dumb Society of NSW, 1971. 12p.

(651) QUEENSLAND. Department of Education. Children with special needs; provision for the education of handicapped children in Queensland. Brisb, 1971. 17p.

(652) SPECIFIC Learning Difficulties Association, Victoria. Reading difficulty and the intelligent under-achiever: report of proceedings of a seminar for teachers. Melb, 1971. 42p.

1972 (653) JEANES, D. R. and others. Aid to communication with the deaf. Carlton, Vic, Massina, [1972]. 149p.

(d) Migrants

1936 (654) KINGSLEY Fairbridge Farm School of Western Australia. A description. Perth, 1936. 24p.

1948 (655) FAIRBRIDGE, R. E. Fairbridge Farm: the building of a farm school. Perth, Paterson, 1948. 189p.
First published in Great Britain in 1937 under the title 'Pinjarra'.

1961 (656) QUEENSLAND. Department of Education. Research and Guidance Branch. A survey of migrant children and children of migrants in Queensland state schools, 1959. Brisb, 1961. 30 leaves. (Bulletin no 22).

1970 (657) BASSETT, G. W. Education and the new settler. Canb, Govt Pr, 1970. 21p.

(658) NICHOLS, O. A. The language problems of migrant children. Kingsgrove, NSW, Aust Citizenship Convention, 1970. 14p.

(659) ROPER, T. W. Bibliography of migration to Australia from non-English speaking countries, with special reference to education. Melb, Centre for the Study of Urban Education, School of Education, La Trobe Univ, 1970. 15p.

1971 (660) AUSTRALIAN Frontier. Consultation on the migrant and the school. Malvern, Vic, 1971. 39p.

(661) NEW South Wales. Department of Education. Division of Research and Planning. Migrant education in New South Wales, prepared by C. Von Sturmer. Syd, 1971. 77p. (Research Bulletin, no 34).

(662) SMOLICZ, J. J. and Wiseman, R. European migrants and their children; interaction, assimilation, education. Hawthorn, Vic, ACER, 1971. 2 vols (Quarterly Review of Australian Education, vol 4 nos 2 & 3).

(663) TWO worlds: school and the migrant family. North Melb, Stockland, 1971. 70p. (A Project of the Brotherhood of St Laurence).

(664) VICTORIA. Education Department. Some findings on the role of language in the acquisition of operational structures; performance on Piagetian Conservation tasks by bilingual Greek children, by G. Gallagher. Melb, 1971. 20p. (RR 5/71).

(665) AUSTRALIAN Frontier. The migrant in the community: Part 1. A survey by P. M. Oliver; Part 2. Consultation [with papers by] M. P. Tsounis and P. M. Oliver. Malvern, Vic, 1972. 2 vols.

(e) Rural Education

1914 (666) SMYTH, J. The rural school in Australia; its theory and practice with an exposition of some modern ideals and principles. Melb, G. Robertson, [1914?] . 452p.

1926 (667) ELIJAH, J. W. The rural school; its problems and functions. Melb, R & M, 1926. 152p.

1931 (668) CUNNINGHAM, K. S. Primary education by correspondence; being an account of the methods and achievements of the Australian correspondence schools in instructing children living in isolated areas. Melb, MUP, 1931. 91p. (ACER Educational Research Series, no 3).

1935 (669) LEWIS, C. G. Education for sparsley populated areas, with special reference to the correspondence school. Adel, Education Dept, 1935. (Bulletin no 3).

1937 (670) COLE, P. R. , editor. The rural school in Australia. Melb, MUP, 1937. 244p. (ACER Educational Research Series, no 49). 'The present report is not only an attempt at the systematic and scientific examination of rural education in Australia, but it is also a revelation of the experience and theories of a number of our leading educationists' (introduction).
Contents: The Australian environment: a brief survey by R. G. Cameron; The psychology of the rural child by H. T. Lovell; Rural school administration by F. Tate; Buildings and equipment by K. S. Cunningham; School activities and methods of study by H. T. Parker; Courses of study by G. A. Osborne; The time-table and other special problems by J. M. Braithwaite and C. R. McRae; Statistics by H. S. Wyndham.

1938 (671) SYDNEY Technical College. Correspondence Teaching
Division. International Conference on Correspondence Instruction
to be held in Victoria, British Columbia, August 1938; material
for pre-convention bulletin. Syd, Dept of Education, 1938. 10
leaves.

1939 (672) RADFORD, W. C. The educational needs of a rural community. Melb, MUP, 1939. 183p. (ACER Educational Research
Series, no 56).

1945 (673) MALING, F. M. Rural education: the case for the country
college. Wongan Hills, WA, Wongan Hills Roads Board, 1945.
16p.

1947 (674) AUSTRALIAN Council for Educational Research. Australian
correspondence school questionnaire. Melb, 1947. 24 leaves.

1948 (675) KENNA, J. C. and Hopkins, H. W. The experimental rural
school, Errol Street, North Melbourne; report. Melb, ACER,
1948. 54 leaves.

1949 (676) RAYNER, S. A., compiler. Correspondence education in
Australia and New Zealand. Melb, MUP, 1949. 119p. (ACER
Educational Research Series, no 64).
A revision of 'Primary education by correspondence' (1931), entry 668

1956 (677) THE SHIRE of Ferntree Gully and its educational future; a
report compiled by ACER, University of Melbourne Faculty of
Education and the Victorian Education Department. Melb, ACER,
1956. 95p.

1960 (678) NEW South Wales. Department of Technical Education.
Correspondence Teaching Division. Golden jubilee. Syd, 1960.
32p.

1963 (679) CAMPBELL, W. J. Growing up in Karribee; a study of child
growth and development in an Australian rural community. Melb,
ACER, 1963. 165p. (Educational Research Series, no 77).

1964 (680) REIDY, D. It's this way. Melb, Heinemann, 1964. 193p.
Novel about a young teacher in a bush primary school.

1967 (681) EDUCATION Seminar, Kerang, Victoria, 1967. Education
problems of the country child. Melb, Victorian Council of School
Organisations, 1967. 22 leaves.

(682) ERDOS, R. F. Teaching by correspondence. Lond, Longmans,
1967. 218p. (A Unesco Source Book).

1969 (683) EDUCATION Seminar, Kyabram High School, Victoria, 1969.
Education problems of the country child. Melb, Victorian Council of
School Organisations, 1969. 13 leaves.

1971 (684) ASHTON, J. Out of the silence: [Australia's schools of the
air]. Adel, Investigation Press, 1971. 221p.

3   Education in Practice (2)

This chapter contains sections on (i) higher education; (ii) teaching methods in higher education; (iii) universities; (iv) research; (v) teacher education; (vi) colleges of advanced education; (vii) vocational education.

(i) Higher Education

1961 (685) MERRYLEES, W. A. Never mind the country: an examination of the first report of the (NSW) Committee on Higher Education. Goolgowi, NSW, Riverine University League, 1961. 12p.

(686) MERRYLEES, W. A. Submission to the Committee on Tertiary Education in Victoria. Goolgowi, NSW, Riverine University League, 1961. 25p.

1962 (687) SUBMISSIONS to the Committee on Australian Tertiary Education. Melb, ACER, 1962-64. 2 documents.
[Document no 1]. What proportion of an age group could undertake tertiary education (or some defined form of tertiary education) with prospects of successful completion? by M. L. Turner; Document no 2. What should universities be able to assume about the qualifications of matriculants and how can these expectations be met by secondary schools? by W. C. Radford.

1963 (688) MERRYLEES, W. A. The city, universities; the country, colleges. Carrathool, NSW, Riverine University League, 1963. 25p.

1965 (689) AUSTRALIAN Institute of Political Science. Summer School, 31st, Canberra, 1965. Tertiary education in Australia; [papers. Edited by J. Wilkes. Syd,] A & R, 1965. 202p.
Contents: Tertiary education: society and the future by P. H. Partridge; The universities by Lord Bowden; The technical colleges by H. S. Williams; The informal education system by L. Wilson; Politics and resources for tertiary education by A. Hall and S. Encel.

(690) WHEELWRIGHT, E. L. , editor. Higher education in Australia. Melb, Cheshire for the Federation of Aust Univ Staff Assns, 1965. 431p.

1966 (691) AUSTRALIA. Minister for Works (J. G. Gorton). Tertiary education; statement by Minister in charge of Commonwealth activities in education and research, the Senate, 21st September 1966. [Canb, Dept of Works?, 1966]. 44p.

1967 (692) DAVIE, R. S. Structure of engineering diplomas; views of recent graduates. Hawthorn, Vic, Swinburne Technical College, 1967. 11p.

(693) HAUGHTON, J. A survey on the demand and opportunities for agricultural and veterinary education for women in Australia. Melb, Univ of Melb School of Agriculture, 1967. 9p.

(694) LAW, P. The changing pattern of requirements in professional education. Melb, College of Nursing, Australia, 1967. 6p. (Chomley Oration, no 1).

(695) PAPUA New Guinea University Library. Higher education in the Territory. Boroko, TPNG, 1967. 4p. (New Guinea Bibliography, no 1).
Articles published since the report of the Commission on Higher Education in Papua and New Guinea. (1964).

1968 (696) OPPORTUNITY in education. Carlton, Vic, Aust College of Education, 1968. 169p.
Papers presented at the 9th Annual Conference, 1968 of the Australian College of Education.
Contents: The accountability of universities by Sir J. Crawford; Opportunity for professional advancement by L. N. Short; Opportunity and diversity in tertiary education by C. Sanders; Development of tertiary courses in Victorian technical colleges by A. E. Lambert; Opportunity for degrees for teachers by D. M. McDonell; An examination of equality of opportunity in education in relation to rural and city children in NSW by D. J. A. Verco and L. A. Whiteman; Opportunities in SA secondary schools by D. J. Anders; External study: a vital component at all levels of an education system by H. C. Pratt; The drop-out phenomenon by P. Chopra; The pursuit of excellence: an Australian fiction by I. V. Hansen; Educational opportunity in a centralized system of education by A. W. Jones; Authority and opportunity in Catholic education by N. W. Cook; Conference review by W. N. Oats.

(697) RESPONSIBILITIES of universities and of employers for professional training. Brisb, Univ of Qld, [1968?]. 51p.
Papers presented during a conference of appointment officers and student counsellors of Australian Universities held at the University of Queensland, Friday 16 August 1968.

(698) WYNDHAM, H. S. Education in a computer world. Syd, NSW Branch, Australian Computer Society, 1968. 19p.

1969 (699) AUSTRALIAN Association of Occupational Therapists. Educational objectives for students of occupational therapy in Australia. Oakleigh, Vic, 1969. 12p.

(700) AUSTRALIAN Association of Occupational Therapists. Occupational therapy education in Australia; clinical practice. Oakleigh, Vic, 1969. 12p.

(701) CONFERENCE on Planning in Higher Education, University of New England, 1969. Papers. Armidale, Univ of New England in association with NUAUS, 1969. 1 vol (various pagination).

(702) DUNN, S. S. and others. A study of the choice of tertiary education by 5th and 6th form males in Victoria. Clayton, Vic, Faculty of Education, Monash Univ, 1969. 191p.
Sponsored by the Commonwealth Advisory Committee on Advanced Education.

(703) NEW directions in tertiary education; public symposium: papers . Nedlands, WA, Univ of WA, [1969?]. 1 vol (various pagination).

1971 (704) PAPUA New Guinea. Manpower Planning Unit. Office of Programming and Co-ordination. Institutional training in Papua New Guinea; statistical compendium. Port Moresby, 1971. 2 vols.

(705) PETERS, H. Planning and management in tertiary education; report on study tour: cost effectiveness in colleges of advanced education. South Bentley WA, WA Inst of Technology, 1971. 163p.

1972 (706) HARMAN, G. S. and Selby Smith, C. Australian higher education; problems of a developing system. Syd A & R, 1972. 196p.

(707) HIGHES, C. A. The Murray Report fifteen years after; a working paper for the August 1972 meeting of the Federation of Australian University Staff Associations. [Syd?], 1972. 48 leaves, and 5 leaf appendix.

(708) McMULLEN, R. D. Tertiary education in Victoria; a case for consolidation and rationalisation. Melb, VICSAC, 1972. 26p.

(709) PAPUA New Guinea. Manpower Planning Unit. Office of Programming and Co-ordination. Institutional training in Papua New Guinea; a statistical summary. Port Moresby, 1972. 41 leaves. (Manpower Studies, no 6).

(710) SHORT, L. N. Universities and colleges of advanced education; defining the difference. [A working paper for the August 1972 meeting of the Federation of Australian University Staff Associations. Syd?], 1972. 21 leaves.

(ii) Teaching Methods in Higher Education

See subject index for other works on methods of teaching.

1963 (711) AUSTRALIAN Vice-Chancellors Committee. Teaching methods in Australian universities; report based on a survey conducted by a committee appointed by the Australian Vice-Chancellors Committee. (Chairman: J. A. Passmore). [Melb?], 1963. 227p.

1967 (712) SEMINAR on University Teaching, Australian National
University, 1967. Papers given at the Seminar on University
Teaching held at ... Canberra, 21-23 February 1967. Canb,
Dept of Adult Education ANU, 1967. 62p.

(713) SYMPOSIUM on Computer Assisted Instruction, University
of New South Wales, 1967. Report, edited by D. V. Connor. Syd,
1967. 23p.
Sponsored jointly by the Educational Research Unit and the Department of Electronic Computation, University of NSW.

1968 (714) KANEFF, S. and Vladcoff, A. N. Self-organising teaching
systems. Canb, Dept of Engineering Physics, Research School
of Physical Sciences, ANU, 1968. 39 leaves.

(715) NATIONAL Union of Australian University Students. Education Department. Teaching and learning in the university. Melb,
1968. 7 leaves.
Introduction by T. Roper; article on the Centre for the Study of
Higher Education in the University of Melbourne by B. Falk.

1969 (716) ROPER, T. W. , editor. Some aspects of university teaching
and learning. North Melb, NUAUS, 1969. 29 leaves.

1971 (717) FALK, B. and Lee Dow, K. University teaching; reality
and change. Hawthorn, Vic, ACER, 1971. 58p. (Quarterly
Review of Australian Education, vol 4 no 4).

1972 (718) WIDDEN, M. B. Some aspects of university teaching in the
USA and New Zealand. Nedlands, WA, Research Unit in University
Education, Univ of WA, 1972. 12 leaves.

(iii) Universities

1935 (719) KEPPEL, F. P. and Priestley, R. E. The living university;
two addresses delivered at the annual commencement, 1935. Melb,
MUP, 1935. 28p.
Contents: The university today, by F. P. Keppel; The university
ideal, by R. E. Priestley.

1936 (720) HART, A. University reform and finance; what is and what
should be. Melb, MUP, 1936. 128p.

1937 (721) AUSTRALIAN and New Zealand Universities Conference,
Adelaide, 1937. Report of proceedings. Adel, Univ of Adel,
1937. 136p.

(722) PRIESTLEY, R. E. The university and national life; three
addresses to political organisations. Melb, MUP, 1937. 48p.

1938 (723) NEW England University College. University education in
New South Wales and the New England University College. Armidale,
1938. 12p.

1939 (724) MENZIES, R. G. The place of a university in the modern community: an address delivered at the annual commencement of the Canberra University College, 1939. Melb, MUP, 1939. 32p.

1943 (725) BOOTH, E. H. Decentralisation of university education. Armidale, NSW, the Author, 1943. 16p.

1944 (726) ASHBY, E. Universities in Australia. Melb, ACER, 1944. 34p. (Future of Education Series, no 5).

1945 (727) MEDLEY, J. D. G. The present and future of Australian universities. Melb, MUP, 1945. 45p. (John Murtagh Macrossan Lectures, 1945).

(728) MITCHELL, F. W. Student health: [an address]. Adel, Univ of Adel, 1945. 15p.

1947 (729) HAWKEN, R. W. H. The university and the professions. Brisb, Univ of Qld, 1946. 31p. (John Thomson Lecture, 1935).

(730) MATRICULATION requirements at Australian, New Zealand and some English and Scottish universities. Melb, ACER, 1947. 17 leaves. (Information Bulletin, no 8).

(731) SANDERS, C. Student selection and the universities; [paper presented to the] Australian and New Zealand Association for the Advancement of Science, Section J, Perth 1947. Perth, ANZAAS, 1947. 4p.

1950 (732) AUSTRALIA. Commonwealth Office of Education. Information concerning institutions of higher learning. Syd, Govt Pr, 1950. 83p.

(733) PAGE, Sir E. The value of decentralisation of university education in Australia. Canb, Canb Univ College, 1950. 14p.

1952 (734) AUSTRALIAN Vice-Chancellors Committee. A crisis in the finances and development of the Australian universities. Melb, MUP, 1952. 18p.

1953 (735) MERRYLEES, W. A. The case for an Australian rural university. Carathool NSW, Riverine University League, 1953. 60p.
Second edition published in 1957.

1954 (736) WORKERS Educational Association of New South Wales. Universities of New South Wales: proceedings of a convention on the past pattern and future trends, Sydney, 24-27 September 1954. Syd, 1957. 88p.

1955 (737) SYMPOSIUM on the place of the Australian university in the community and post-graduate studies in the Australian universities. Melb, Australian Vice-Chancellors Committee, 1955. 66p. Papers delivered in August 1955 during a Commonwealth inter-university conference arranged in Australia by the Association of Universities of the British Commonwealth and the Australian Vice-Chancellors Committee.

1957 (738) AUSTRALIAN Vice-Chancellors Committee. Submission by the Australian Vice-Chancellors Committee to the Committee on Australian Universities, 4 July 1957. Carlton, Vic, MUP, 1957. 36p.

(739) MERRYLEES, W. A. A countryman's appreciation of the Murray Report. Hay, NSW, the Author, 1957. 7p.

(740) SYDNEY Association of University Teachers. Submission to the Commonwealth government Committee of Enquiry into the future of Australian universities. Syd, 1957. 29p.

1958 (741) TASMANIA. University. The dismissal of S.S. Orr by the University of Tasmania; issued by the Vice-Chancellor with the authority of the Council of the University of Tasmania. Hobart, 1958. 54p.

1959 (742) PRICE, A. G. , editor. The humanities in Australia; a survey with special reference to the universities. Syd, A & R for the Aust Humanities Research Council, 1959. 337p.

(743) SOME problems of university education; report of proceedings of Staff Seminar, University of New South Wales, 11-12 November 1959. Syd, NSW University Educational Research Section, 1959. 160p.
Contents: Aims and methods in university teaching, by W. H. Frederick and D. W. Phillips; The student and his needs by R. Priestley and G. Gray; University examinations by S. S. Dunn and L. N. Short; Matriculation and student selection by I. G. Meddleton and F. J. Clark.

1960 (744) ROWE, A. P. If the gown fits. Melb, MUP, 1960. 240p.

(745) SANDERS, C. The problems of first-year failure in Australian universities. Perth Univ of WA, 1960. 7p.
Summary of address given to the Western Australian Institute for Educational Research, 9 August 1960.

1961 (746) ARBLASTER, H. E. Proposal for extension of university education in Victorian country areas through the School of Mines and Industries, Ballarat, submitted to the Committee for Development of Tertiary Education in Victoria by the Council of the School of Mines and Industries, Ballarat, 19 October, 1961. Ballarat, Vic, 1961. 15p.

(747) APPS, B. F. G. , compiler. Australian and New Zealand university health services; a report of the first seminar, Adelaide, SA, September 1960. Adel, Univ Union Health Service Committee, 1960. 20p.

(748) CONFERENCE on university education, University of Melbourne, 1960. Report. Melb, 1961. 72p.
'Conference called by the Australian Vice-Chancellors Committee. Report for use only within universities' (note in Australian National Bibliography, 1961).

(749) CONFERENCE of Australian universities, University of Sydney, 1961. Report and proceedings. Melb, Univ Book-room, 1961. 174p.
Convened by the Australian Vice-Chancellors' Committee in co-operation with the Federal Council of University Staff Associations of Australia.

(750) SANDERS, C. Psychological and educational bases of academic performance. Melb, ACER, 1961. 179p. (Educational Research Series, no 74).

(751) SYMPOSIUM on the Australian Universities 1970, University of New South Wales, Sydney, 6-7 December 1960. Papers presented. Syd, Univ of NSW, 1961. 80p.

1962 (752) ARBLASTER, H. E. Contribution to the solution of problems confronting the development of Australian university education, submitted to the Commonwealth Committee on the Future of Tertiary Education by the Ballarat School of Mines and Industries, 19 February 1962. Ballarat, Vic, 1962. 26p.

(753) JOHNSTON, F. H. Report on leave of absence, by the Registrar (F. H. Johnston). Melb, Univ of Melb, 1962. 9p.
Deals with university administration.

(754) MERRYLEES, W. A. Submissions to expert committees, with two addenda. Carrathool, NSW, Riverine University League, 1962. 132p.

(755) MERRYLEES, W. A. Universities as the basis of balanced development. Carrathool, NSW, Riverine University League, 1962. 10p.

(756) SCHOOLS and Universities Conference, University of Melbourne, 1962, attended by secondary school representatives and members of the staff of the University of Melbourne and the Monash University on 22 May. Melb, Univ Appointments Board, 1962. 74p.

1963 (757) MERRYLEES, W. A. The universities we need. Carrathool, NSW, Riverine University League, 1963. 22p.

1964 (758) AUSTRALASIAN Association of Philosophy. Executive. Report to the AAP Council on the moves for a settlement of the Orr case. Syd, 1964. 85p.

(759) BRODSKY, I. Let no dog bark. Syd, Old Syd Free Press, 1964. 95p.
'This work concerns itself with some vital university issues'.

(760) CONFERENCE of Australian Universities, University of Melbourne. 1964. Report of proceedings. Melb, MUP, 1964. 220p.
Convened by the Australian Vice-Chancellors Committee. Conference theme: Student residence in Australian universities.

(761) MENZIES, Sir R.G. The universities: some queries. Syd, Univ of NSW, 1964. 23p. (Wallace Wurth Memorial Lecture, 1st, 1964).

(762) MERRYLEES, W.A. The academically under-privileged, a reply to the Minister for Education's statement of reasons for putting a third university in Sydney. Carrathool, NSW, Riverine University League, 1964. 14p.

(763) MERRYLEES, W.A. A concise statement of the case for a Riverine rural university. Carrathool, NSW, Riverine University League, 1964. 8p.

(764) MERRYLEES, W.A. Co-operate or fail; an examination of the new degree-granting educational facilities in Victoria, as proposed in June 1964. Carrathool, NSW, Riverine University League, 1964. 16p.

(765) MULLINS, R. Proposal; the Irish-Australian Cultural University, Melbourne. Melb, the Author, 1964. 8p.

(766) PHILP, H., and others. The university and its community. Syd, Novak, 1964. 174p.
Contributors are R.L. Debus; V. Veidemanis; W.F. Connell.

(767) ROWLEY, S. School and university scholarships. Syd, NSW Branch of the Economic Society of Aust. and NZ, 1964. 11p.

1965 (768) CAIDEN, N. A bibliography for Australian universities. Canb, ANU, 1965. 75p.

(769) DAVIES, G.N. Precept and practice in the university; education or vocational training. Brisb, Univ of Qld Press, 1965. 18p. (Queensland University. Inaugural lectures).

(770) McMANNERS, J. and Crawford, R.M. The future of the humanities in the Australian universities. Melb, MUP for Aust Humanities Research Council, 1965. 32p.

(771) MERRYLEES, W.A. City sorcery; an examination of the Martin Report as it affects the Riverine area. Carrathool, NSW, Riverine University League, 1965. 56p.

(772) SYMPOSIUM on the University and Industry, University of New South Wales, 1964. Papers presented. Syd Univ of NSW, 1965. 63p.

1966 (773) AUSTIN, M.N. An ignorant man thinking; essays and addresses. Nedlands WA, Univ of WA Press, 1966. 254p.

(774) MERRYLEES, W.A. Riverine University College; a critical discussion of the relevant sections of the third report of the Australian Universities Commission and Senator Gorton's statement thereon. Carrathool, NSW, Riverine University League, 1966. 12p.

(775) POWELL, J.P., compiler. Universities and university education; a select bibliography. Slough, Bucks, National Foundation for Educational Research in England and Wales, 1966. 59p. (NFER Occasional Publication, no 14).

(776) SYMPOSIUM on the Role of the University in Preparation for the Professions, University of New South Wales, 1966. Proceedings. Kensington, NSW, Univ of NSW, 1966. 61p.

1967 (777) ATKINS, R. , editor. University government; proceedings of a seminar held in Canberra, June 1965 under the auspices of the Federation of Australian University Staff Associations. Syd, the Federation, [1967]. 87p.

(778) COMMONWEALTH Scientific and Industrial Research Organisation. Committee on relationship between CSIRO and the Universities. Report. [Melb?] , CSIRO Advisory Council, 1967. 13 leaves.

(779) INTER-UNIVERSITY Conference on Part-time Teaching in Australian Universities, University of Queensland, 1967. Proceedings. Brisb, Dept of External Studies, Univ of Qld, 1967. 64p.

(780) LANGUAGES and the Community Committee. Why learn foreign languages? [Syd, Univ of NSW, 1967?] . 1 vol (various pagination).

(781) MELBOURNE. University. Appointments Board. Scholarships, cadetships and other forms of financial assistance available to university students. Parkville, Vic, 1968. 49p.

(782) MERRYLEES, W. A. Still no light; an examination of the Australian Universities Commission's report on tertiary facilities in the Riverina. Carrathool, NSW, Riverine University League, 1967. 32p.

(783) SHORT, L. N. What do we teach? An essay in the analysis of the content of university teaching. Kensington, NSW, Educational Research Unit, Univ of NSW, 1967. 13p. (Occasional Publication no 5).

(784) WALKER, W. G. , editor. School to university. Armidale, NSW, Dept of Education, Univ of New England, 1967. 95p. (New England Papers on Education, no 2).
A report of the proceedings of the High School Principal's Conference held at the University of New England from 31 May to 2 June 1967.

1968 (785) CARTLAND, Sir G. The university and the modern world. Hobart, Univ of Tasmania, 1968. 26p. (University of Tasmania Inaugural Lecture).

(786) COMMONWEALTH Universities Congress, 10th, Sydney 1968. Tenth Commonwealth Universities Congress, Sydney, 17-23 August 1968. Syd, Assn of Commonwealth Univs, 1968. 15p.

(787) LAWLOR, J. , editor. The new university. Lond, Routledge & Kegan Paul, 1968. 200p.

(788) MACMILLAN, D. S. Australian universities; a descriptive sketch. Syd, Syd Univ Pr for Aust Vice-Chancellors Committee, 1968. 111p.

(789) MATHESON, J. A. L. Problems of Australian universities. Melb, Alfred Deakin Lecture Trust, 1968. 19p. (Alfred Deakin Lecture, no 2, 1968).

(790) SCHONELL, Sir F. J. The university in contemporary society. Canb, Assn of Commonwealth Univs, 1968. 22p. Address given at Tenth Commonwealth Universities Congress, Sydney, 17-23 August 1968.

1969 (791) THE COLLEGE of the 70s Conference, University of Sydney, 1969. Report of the National Association of Australian University Colleges. Camperdown, NSW, NAAUC, 1969. 59 leaves.

(792) CONFERENCE on the Role and Responsibilities of Governing Bodies, Australian National University, Canberra 1969. [Papers]. Canb, 1969. 1 vol (various pagination).

(793) CONGRESS of the Universities of the Commonwealth, 10th Sydney 1968. Report of proceedings, edited by T. Craig, Lond, Assn of Commonwealth Univs, 1969. 488p.

(794) ROPER, T. W. A proposal for a higher education fees concession scheme. North Melb, NUAUS, 1969. 24 leaves.

(795) ROPER, T. W. The rises in university fees. North Melb, NUAUS, 1969. 14 leaves.

1970 (796) COCHRANE, D. Report to Australian Vice-Chancellors Committee on Year-Round Teaching. Canb, Aust Vice-Chancellors Committee, 1970. 64p.

(797) COMMONWEALTH Tertiary Scholarship schemes; review by NUAUS. North Melb, NUAUS, 1970. 39p.

(798) COWEN, Z. Some thoughts on the Australian universities. Canb, Royal Inst of Public Administration (ACT Group), 1970. 12p. (Robert Garran Memorial Oration, 23rd, Canberra 1970).

(799) DE FOSSARD, R. A. B. , editor. A university perspective. Syd, Wiley, 1970. 203p.
'Our aim ... is to present some insight into a sample of the range of disciplines offered by most universities' (preface).

(800) HOW efficient are Australian universities? Papers presented at the symposium held at the University of New South Wales on 7 November 1969. Kensington, NSW, Univ of NSW, 1970. 67p.

(801) LITTLE, F. G. The university experience; an Australian study. Carlton, Vic, MUP, 1970. 247p.

(802) ROPER, T. W. Abolition of tertiary education fees. North Melb, NUAUS, 1970. 12p.

(803) SYDNEY. University. Liberal Club. The present crisis in the universities; a report. Syd, 1970. 23p.

1972 (804) CUTT, J. Program budgeting and higher education: a review of the state of the art. Canb, Dept of Accounting and Public Finance, ANU, 1972. 151p. (Public Finance Monographs, no 1).

(805) FLETCHER, N. H. The role of the university in society. [Univ of Syd, 1972]. 13 leaves.
Paper presented at the Sixth Annual Meeting of the Australian University Graduate Conference, Hobart, January 1972.

(806) GEORGE, D. W. Report to the Federation of Australian University Staff Associations on academic staff structure and university government in Australian universities. [Syd?], the Federation, 1972. 51p.

(807) SOLOMON, R. J. The role of the university in society as seen by the government. [Univ of Syd, 1972]. 7 leaves.

(808) VALENTINE, R. The role of the university in society as seen by the community. [Univ of Syd, 1972]. 12 leaves.

Descriptive works such as histories or special studies concerned with individual universities, or aspects of a university, are included in the following section, arranged under the name of the university. Regularly updated publications (such as calendars, handbooks, guides, research reports, statistical reports) are omitted.

See also pages 62-63 which include material on teaching methods in universities.

Australian National University

1952 (809) AUSTRALIAN National University, Canberra. The Australian National University: a brief description of the development of the University from its foundation in 1946. Canb, 1952. 23p.

1953 (810) FLOREY, Sir H. W. The John Curtin School of Medical Sciences, the Australian National University. Canb, ANU, 1953. 21p.

1965 (811) JEANNERET, M. Report on scholarly publishing at the Australian National University. Canb, ANU, 1965. 116p.

1968 (812) CRAWFORD, Sir J. G. The Australian National University; its concept and role. Canb, ANU, 1968. 24p.
An address to the Convocation of the University of Melbourne given on 29 March 1968.

Flinders University

1964 (813) STEPHENSON, G. and Harrison, G. J. The University of Adelaide at Bedford Park; site planning report. Adel, Univ of Adel at Bedford Park, 1964. 58p.
Later called Flinders University, Bedford Park.

La Trobe University

1967 (814) MYERS, D. M. A new university in a changing world. Melb, Cheshire for La Trobe Univ, 1967. 15p. (Inaugural Lectures Series).

Macquarie University

1969 (815) MEYER, G. R. Policies and activities; a report of the first thirty months (January 1967 to June 1969) of the Macquarie University Centre for Advancement of Teaching . North Ryde, NSW, Macquarie Univ, 1969. 20p.

Monash University

1968 (816) BLACKWOOD, Sir R. R. Monash University: the first ten years. Melb, Hampden Hall, 1968. 262p.

1969 (817) MONASH University, Melbourne. Commission on University Affairs. Recommendations, together with a statement by some members. Clayton, Vic, 1969. 9p.

1970 (818) MONASH University. Monash and the community. Clayton, Vic, 1970. 52p.

University of Adelaide

1936 (819) ADELAIDE. University. St Mark's College: the history of the college, and college register, 1925-35. Adel, 1936. 25p. Special supplement to St Mark's College Record.

(820) ADELAIDE. University. Conversazione in honour of the state centenary celebrations and of the sixtieth anniversary of the University. Adel, 1936. 23p.

1968 (821) PRICE, Sir G. A history of St Mark's College, University of Adelaide and the foundation of the residential college movement. Adel, Council of St Mark's College, 1968. 126p.

University of Melbourne

1936 (822) SCOTT, E. A history of the University of Melbourne. Melb, MUP, 1936. 246p.

1952 (823) CRAWFORD, R. M. Wilson Hall; centre and symbol of the University. Melb, MUP, 1952. 22p.

1956 (824) BLAINEY, G. The University of Melbourne; a centenary portrait. Melb, MUP, 1956. 184p.

(825) MELBOURNE. University. The University of Melbourne centenary celebrations, 14 August to 16 August 1956. Melb, MUP, 1957. 77p.

1957 (826) BLAINEY, G. A centenary history of the University of Melbourne. Melb, MUP, 1957. 229p.

1960 (827) NASH, L.L. Forward flows the time: [the story of] Ridley
College, Melbourne. Melb, GB Publications, 1960. 226p.
Ridley College is a residential college at the University of Melbourne.

1964 (828) JOSKE, E. Recollections of Janet Clarke Hall. Melb, the
Author, 1964. 30p.
Janet Clarke Hall is the oldest of all the university women's colleges
in Australia. It was established in 1886.

(829) MELBOURNE. University. Students Representative Council.
Melbourne University: a student report; memorandum to the
Council of the University of Melbourne. Melb, 1964. 21p.

1970 (830) MELBOURNE. University. Staff Association. The implications for the University of Melbourne of the fourth report of the
Australian Universities Commission. Melb, 1970. 6 leaves.

University of New England

1959 (831) DRUMMOND, D. H. A university is born; the story of the
founding of the University College of New England. Syd, A & R,
1959. 143p.

1965 (832) SHEATH, H. C. External studies; the first ten years,
1955-64. Armidale, NSW, Univ of New England, 1965. 44p.

University of New South Wales

1961 (833) BAXTER, J. P. Address delivered on 28 April 1961 to
commemorate the services of Wallace Charles Wurth to the
University. Text written by J.P. Baxter and J.O.A. Bourke.
Syd, Univ of NSW, 1961. 28p.

University of Papua and New Guinea

1968 (834) HARRISON, G. J. The University of Papua and New Guinea;
site planning report. [Port Moresby, Univ of PNG, 1968?]. 32p.

1969 (835) PAPUA New Guinea. University. Educational Materials
Centre. Development, progress and planned activities of the
Educational Materials Centre at the University of Papua and New
Guinea. Boroko, TPNG, 1969. 30p.

University of Queensland

1957 (836) ROBINSON, F. W. The University of Queensland, St Lucia,
Brisbane. Brisb, Qld Univ, 1957. 32p.

1964 (837) LOCKLEY, G. L. Grads and undergrads and fellows;
Cromwell College, the University of Queensland, 1950- 64.
Brisb, Cromwell College, 1964. 57p.

(838) UP the right channels. St Lucia, Univ of Qld, 1970. 243p.
A critical evaluation of the University of Queensland: 'This book
was compiled as a result of a number of people within the University
coming together at a meeting'.

University of Sydney

1938 (839) DALLEN, R. The University of Sydney: its history and
progress from its foundation in 1852 to 1938, together with short
biographical sketches of its ten chancellors. [3rd ed]. Syd, A & R,
1938. 62p.

1940 (840) BAVIN, Sir T. R., editor. The jubilee book of the Law
School of the University of Sydney, 1890-1940. Syd, Law School,
Univ of Syd, 1940. 280p.

1946 (841) ANDERSON, D. J. Some of the history of the Sydney University
Union. Syd, A'sian Medical Pub Co, 1946. 10p.

1947 (842) ROBINSON, F. W. The Great Hall of the University of Sydney
and voices of the past. Syd, Syd Univ Extension Board, 1947.
22p.

1952 (843) ONE hundred years of the Faculty of Arts; a series of
commemorative lectures given in the Great Hall, University of
Sydney, during April and May 1952. Syd, A & R,1952. 80p.

(844) SYDNEY. University. Office of Information and Public
Relations. Centenary celebrations, August 26-31 1952. Syd,
1952. 99p.

(845) SYDNEY. University. Union. The Union book of 1952,
being the contribution of the Sydney University Union to the cele-
bration of the centenary of the University of Sydney. Syd, 1952.
189p.

1953 (846) HOLE, W. V. and Treweeke, A. H. History of the Women's
College within the University of Sydney. Syd, Halstead Press,
1953. 220p.

1964 (847) DOUGAN, A. A., compiler. The Andrew's book, being a
book about St Andrew's College within the University of Sydney.
Syd, St Andrew's College, 1964. 110p.

(848) SYDNEY. University. Office of the Assistant Principal.
The redevelopment of the University extension area. Syd, 1964.
21p.

1968 (849) GAMBLE, A. The University of Sydney. Syd, Univ of Syd,
1968. 1 vol (unpaged).

1969 (850) MACMILLAN, D. S. Charles Nicholson. Melb, OUP, 1969.
30p. (Great Australians).
Nicholson was speaker of the first Legislative Council of NSW, and
active in the founding of the University of Sydney.

University of Tasmania

1970 (851) TASMANIA. University. The University of Tasmania, 1890-1970. Hobart, 1970. 23p.

University of Western Australia

1963 (852) ALEXANDER, F. Campus at Crawley; a narrative and critical appreciation of the first fifty years of the University of Western Australia. Melb, Cheshire for the Univ of WA Press, 1963. 895p.

1971 (853) ALEXANDER, F. The University of Western Australia; its buildings and grounds. Nedlands, WA, Univ of WA, 1971. 24p.

(iv) Research

Research publications on particular aspects of education have been included with the entries for the subjects (e. g. Mathematics).

1940 (854) AUSTRALIAN Council for Educational Research. Educational studies and investigations; summaries of investigations submitted in 1936-39 by students in the second year of the course for Bachelor of Education degree at the University of Melbourne. Melb, MUP, 1940. 240p.

1945 (855) TRAVELLING scholarships available to Australians for study overseas. Melb, ACER, 1945. 6 leaves. (Information Bulletin, no 1).

1953 (856) AUSTRALIAN Council for Educational Research. Theses in education and educational psychology accepted for degrees at Australian universities, 1919-50. Melb, 1953. 40p.

1955 (857) AUSTRALIAN Council for Educational Research. A record of Council activities, 1930-55. Melb, 1955. Melb, 1955. 43p.

1956 (858) INTERNATIONAL Conference on Educational Research, First, Atlantic City, NJ, 13-21 February 1956: [report]. Melb, ACER, 1956. 27 leaves. (Information Bulletin, no 34).

1957 (859) MELBOURNE. University. Education Library. Bachelor of Education investigations and Master of Education theses held in the Education Library, October, 1957. Melb, 1957. 25p.

1958 (860) UNITED States Educational Foundation in Australia. Fulbright programme in Australia: the first eight years and the future. Canb, 1958. 92p.

1959 (861) MARSHALL, M. J. , editor. Union list of higher degree theses in Australian university libraries. Hobart, Univ of Tas Library, 1959. 237p.
1st Supplement, 1959. 2nd Supplement, 1960.
Cumulative edition to 1965, and supplement 1966-68.

1964 (862) RADFORD, W. C. A field for many tillings; research in education in Australia today. Melb, ACER, 1964. 59p.

1965 (863) HENDERSON, N. K. Statistical research methods in education and psychology. Hong Kong, Univ Press, 1965. 158p.

1966 (864) FITZGERALD, R. T. A system of handling information on Australian education. Hawthorn, Vic, ACER, 1966. 12p. (Memorandum Series, no 3).

(865) SANDERS, C. Educational writing and research in Australia, 1960-65; a bibliographical review. Nedlands, WA, Faculty of Education, Univ of WA, 1966. 73p.

1967 (866) AUSTRALIAN Council for Educational Research. Research into education, improving its value to the practice of education; papers presented at a conference, 18-23 May 1967. Hawthorn, Vic, 1967. 161p.
Contents: The direction and goals of Australian society by P. H. Partridge; Research within a state department of education in Australia by H. S. Wyndham; Research into education: a headmaster's view by B. W. Hone; Educational studies on a new scale in Canada by W. G. Fleming; The Center for Research on Learning and Teaching by S. E. Ericksen; Recruitment, selection and training of personnel for research in Australia by G. D. Bradshaw and G. McK. Brown; Current resources in Australia for research into education, and their effective use by R. Selby Smith; Overcoming limitations to the rapid and effective use of findings by S. B. Hammond and F. N. Cox; A final statement by W. C. Radford.

(867) CUNNINGHAM, K. S. The Social Science Research Council of Australia, 1942-52. Canb, Social Science Research Council, 1967. 34p.

(868) HARVARD Club of Australia. The Harvard Club of Australia announces the Robert Gordon Menzies Scholarship Fund. Syd, the Club, 1967. 12p.

1968 (869) FEDERATION of Australian University Staff Associations. Report on research in universities. Syd, 1968. 46p.

(870) HART, E. K. Directory of philanthropic trusts in Australia. Hawthorn, Vic, ACER, 1968. 289p.

(871) WALKER, W. G. Education in the organisational society; the role of a faculty of education. Armidale, NSW, University of New England, 1968. 27p. (Inaugural Public Lecture).

1970 (872) ANDERSON, J. , Durston, B. H. and Poole, M. Thesis and assignment writing. Syd, Wiley, 1970. 146p.

(873) FARRELL, J. B. Research for teachers. Syd, A & R, 1970. 167p.

(874) MILLER, G. W. Higher education research in Australia and New Zealand; a discussion of the research literature and other studies. Lond, Society for Research into Higher Education, 1970. 65p.

(875) PAPUA New Guinea. Department of Education. Opportunities for research in education and social development in the Territory of Papua and New Guinea. Konedobu, PNG, 1970. 16p.

(876) SEGALL, P. Educational research published in twenty seven Australian journals, 1967-70; an analysis. Melb, ACER, 1970. 13p.

1972 (877) COX, L. A. Analysis of research relevant to colleges of advanced education. [Melb, Victoria Inst of Colleges], 1972. 23 leaves.

(878) SUMNER, R. J. and Lafleur, C. D. Bibliography of educational research and innovation in South Australia. Adel, Education Dept, 1972. 48 leaves.

(v) Teacher Education

1915 (879) MACKIE, A. Training of teachers in New South Wales. Syd, Govt Pr, 1915. 14p.

1939 (880) SWEETMAN, E. History of the Melbourne Teachers College and its predecessors. Melb, MUP, 1939. 144p. (ACER Educational Research Series, no 57).

1943 (881) TURNER, I. S. The training of teachers in Australia; a comparative and critical survey. Melb, ACER, 1943. 504p. (Educational Research Series, no 61).

1955 (882) MOSSENSON, D. A history of teacher training in Western Australia. Melb, ACER, 1955. 126p. (Educational Research Series, no 68).

(883) SANDERS, C. Teacher, school and university; [an address]. Nedlands, WA, Univ of WA Publications Committee, 1955. 24p.

1963 (884) SANDERS, C. and Bassett, G. W. Education as a university study; submission to the Martin Committee on the future of tertiary education in Australia, made at the request of Western Australia, 1963. Nedlands, WA, Univ of WA Faculty of Education, 1963. 39p. 2nd edition, 1967.

1965 (885) QUEENSLAND. Department of Education. Research and Guidance Branch. A comparative study of Queensland teachers college students, 1956 and 1964. Brisb, 1965. 29 leaves. (Bulletin no 26).
See also follow-up study (1970) entry 897, page 77.

(886) TWO cultures; an experiment in learning. [Wollongong, NSW, Wollongong Teachers College, 1965?] . 32p.

1966 (887) NATIONAL Union of Australian University Students. Teacher training and the bond. Melb, 1966. 55p.

1967 (888) HAINES, M. D. Social studies and teacher preparation. Adel, SA Inst of Teachers, [1967?]. 29p.

(889) RICHARDSON, J. A. and Bowen, J., editors. The preparation of teachers in Australia. Melb, Cheshire, 1967. 231p. Contents: The teacher, present and future by A. R. Crane; The content of teacher education by R. Fogarty; The teacher, present and future by D. McLean; Teacher education: some questions from an outsider by S. W. Cohen; The present pattern of teacher education by P. E. Jones; Organisation and government of the education of teachers (i) G. W. Muir; (ii) L. F. Neal and S. D'Urso; The curriculum of a teachers college by L. W. Shears; Implementing the curriculum by L. W. Shears; The American experience: its relevance to Australia by J. Bowen; The British experience: its relevance to Australia by I. S. Turner; The continuing education of teachers by W. D. Neal and D. Mossenson; Preparation of tertiary teachers by B. Falk; The future of teacher education in Australia by J. A. Richardson.

(890) ROWLANDS, E. J. and Fary, N. G. A survey of academic and socio-economic backgrounds of first year studentship holders at Monash Teachers College, Victoria 1967. Melb, Monash Teachers College, 1967. 18 leaves. (Research Report, no 1).

1968 (891) SANDERS, C. Education and the teacher; conference oration. Perth, A'sian Assn of Insts of Inspectors of Schools, 1968. 25p.

(892) SWAN, K. J. Wagga Wagga Teachers College; its site and establishment. Wagga Wagga, NSW, the College, 1968. 31p.

1969 (893) GASTEEN, K., editor. The Diploma of Education course; a report on a national seminar held in Melbourne during December 1967. Melb, NUAUS Education Department, [1969?]. 14 leaves.

1970 (894) FARY, N. G. A survey of the 1969 education year students at Monash Teachers College, Victoria. Melb, Monash Teachers College, 1970. 32p. (Research Report no 3).

(895) GERARD, Sister M. Observations of modern advances in teacher training overseas. Canb, Winston Churchill Memorial Trust, 1970. 32p. (Churchill Information Report, no 7).

(896) NATIONAL Seminar on the Study of Education in Teachers Colleges, 17-22 May 1970. Adel, Division of Teacher Education and Services, Education Dept, 1970. 1 vol (various pagination).

(897) QUEENSLAND. Department of Education. Research and Curriculum Branch. A follow-up study of entrants to courses of teacher education in 1957. Brisb, 1970. 47p. (Bulletin no 38). See also entry 885, page 76.

1971 (898) AUSTRALIA. Committee on Overseas Professional Qualifications. Teacher education in Denmark. Canb, 1971. 31 leaves.
Issues also published on Finland, Germany, Italy, Norway, Sweden,
the Netherlands, the Philippines, Turkey and Yugoslavia.

(899) DOBSON, N. H. Mercer House; the story of the first fifty
years, 1921-71. Melb, Mercer House, 1971. 16p.

1972 (900) WESTERN Australian Tertiary Education Commission.
Preliminary report on the future of the Western Australian Teachers
Colleges. Nedlands, WA, 1972. 23p.

(vi) Colleges of Advanced Education

1967 (901) TASMANIAN College of Advanced Education. Educational
specifications. [Hobart?] , 1967. 155p.
Master plan. Hobart, 1967. 1 vol (unpaged).

1970 (902) BRYAN, H. and Hean, E. L. The function of the library in
a college of advanced education. Syd, [Syd Univ Library?] , 1970.
178p.
Report of a research project conducted for the Commonwealth
Department of Education and Science on the recommendation of
the Commonwealth Advisory Committee on Advanced Education.

(903) FEDERATION of Staff Associations of Australian Colleges
of Advanced Education. Challenges facing advanced education;
report of the 1970 Conference, edited by D. J. Golding and others.
Melb, Hawthorn Press, 1970. 128p.

(904) FEDERATION of Staff Associations of Australian Colleges
of Advanced Education, Warburton Conference, August 1970.
Conference papers. Melb, 1970. 1 vol (various pagination).

(905) HORNE, B. C. and Wise, B. Learning and teaching in the
CAEs, 1969; an objective description of the learning and teaching
situation in the fields of business studies and engineering in the
colleges of advanced education throughout Australia. Hawthorn,
Vic, ACER, 1970. 3 vols.

(906) MADDOX, H. Students entering applied science in colleges
of advanced education; a study of their social origins, educational
background and motivation. Canb, ANU, 1970. 286p. (Research
School of Social Sciences Education Research Unit. Occasional
Report,no 1).

(907) SOUTH Australian Institute of Technology. The role of the
CAEs: the papers, discussions and resolutions of a residential
conference held at Victor Harbour, SA in February 1970, edited
by J. R. Argue. Adel, 1970. 93p.

1971 (908) HORNE, B. C. Aspects of advanced education. Hawthorn,
Vic, ACER, 1971. 56p. (Quarterly Review of Australian Education,
vol 4, no 1).

(909) SKERTCHLY, A. R. B. Policies, roles and planning for
Australian colleges of advanced education; a framework of notes
for discussion. Rockhampton, Capricornia Inst of Advanced
Education, [1971?] . 28p.

1972 (910) AUSTRALIAN Council on Awards in Advanced Education.
Nomenclature and guidelines for awards in advanced education;
statement no 1 Canberra, 1972. 16p.

(vii) Vocational Education

1931 (911) COPLAND, D. B. , editor. Training for business; being a
report of a committee of the Melbourne Chamber of Commerce.
Melb, MUP, 1931. 17p. (ACER Educational Research Series,
no 4).

1947 (912) LENNIE, K. S. Engineering education; [summary of survey].
Melb, ACER, 1947. 3 leaves. (Information Bulletin, no 5).

1954 (913) O'NEILL, W. M. The teaching of psychology in Australia,
the United Kingdom and the United States of America. Melb,
ACER, 1954. 19 leaves.

1959 (914) AUSTRALIAN Institute of Agricultural Science. Agricultural
scientists in Australia; a report. Melb, 1959. 24p.

(915) AUSTRALIAN Institute of Agricultural Science. Victorian
Branch. Submission on agricultural education in secondary and
technical schools. Melb, 1959. 7p.

(916) LLOYD, B. E. The education of professional engineers in
Australia. Melb, Assn of Professional Engineers, Aust, 1959.
490p.
3rd edition 1968.

(917) MOYLE, R. G. , Wadham, Sir S. and Forster, H. C. Submission
on agricultural education in secondary and technical schools to the
Education Committee. Melb, Aust Inst of Agricultural Scientists,
[1959?] . 6 leaves.

1964 (918) COPPLESON, V. M. The development of graduate education
with particular reference to Australia. Syd, Postgraduate Federation
in Medicine, 1964. 46p.

1965 (919) AUSTRALIAN Institute of Agricultural Science. Conference.
3rd, Hobart 1965. Agricultural education; programme, speakers,
papers. Hobart, 1965. 41p.
Held in conjunction with 38th ANZAAS Congress, Section K, 18
August 1965.

(920) CONFERENCE on Postgraduate Medical Education in South and
South-East Asia: Australia's potential contribution, Canberra 1965.
Report. Syd, Postgraduate Federation in Medicine, 1965. 3 vols
in 1.

(921) COTTRELL, T. L. The education of chemists. Syd, Office of Advisory Service, Univ of Syd, 1965. 18p.

1966 (922) AUSTRALIAN College of General Practitioners. Vocational training for general practice and the first College advanced training courses. Melb, 1966. 46p. (ACGP Education Series, no 1).

(923) FARQUHAR, R. N. Agricultural education in Australia. Hawthorn, Vic, ACER, 1966. 332p. (Educational Research Series, no 80).

(924) NALSON, J. S. and Schapper, H. P. Manpower training for agriculture in Western Australia. Nedlands, WA, Univ of WA Press, 1966. 35p.

1967 (925) RUSHOLME, E. J. F. J. , Baron. The education of the scientist in the modern world. Syd, Univ of NSW, [1967?]. 20p. (Wallace Wurth Memorial Lecture, 2nd, 1967).

1968 (926) MELBOURNE Chamber of Commerce. Education, the ally of modern business; symposium, October 22 1968. [Melb, 1968]. 5 parts (various pagination).

1969 (927) AGRICULTURAL education and the community. Syd, Aust Inst of Agricultural Science, 1969. 1 vol (various pagination).

1970 (928) SYMPOSIUM on the educational requirements and needs of aeronautical engineering graduates in Australia in the next decade, Parkville, Victoria 1970. [Papers], compiled and edited by H. K. Millicer. Melb, Royal Aeronautical Society and the Inst of Engineers of Aust, 1970. 1 vol (various pagination).

(929) UNIVERSITY of New England. Tertiary Agricultural Education Project. Consensus and conflict in tertiary agricultural education; a report to the Commonwealth Advisory Committee on Advanced Education and the Commonwealth Department of Primary Industry. Armidale, NSW, 1970. 298p.

(930) VICTORIAN Commercial Teachers Association. Report on research into commercial education. Clifton Hill, Vic, 1970. 123p.

1971 (931) AUSTRALIA. Department of Primary Industry. Survey of trained manpower for Australian agriculture ... 1965/66 to 1974/75. Canb, 1971. 112p.

4   The Process of Education

This chapter contains sections on (i) teachers and teaching; (ii) subject teaching: the humanities, the social sciences, and the natural sciences; (iii) libraries in education; (iv) tests and measurements.

(i) Teachers and Teaching

1926 (932) INSTITUTE of Inspectors of Schools of New South Wales. Teaching and testing. Syd, G. B. Phillip & Son, 1926. 235p.

1931 (933) FOWLER, H. L. Induction or deduction? An experimental investigation in the psychology of teaching. Melb, MUP, 1931. 96p. (ACER Educational Research Series, no 5).

(934) CUNNINGHAM, K. S. and others. The young child; a series of five lectures on child management given under the auspices of the Victorian Council for Mental Hygiene, November 1930. Melb, MUP, 1931. 70p. (ACER Educational Research Series, no 6). Contents: Why children are naughty by K. S. Cunningham; The mischief of fear by J. F. Williams; Should children obey? by M. V. Gutteridge; The child in a temper by G. Springthorpe; The growth of personality by J. A. Gunn.

1932 (935) LUSH, M. and others. The growing child; a series of five lectures on child management given under the auspices of the Victorian Council for Mental Hygiene, October 1931. Melb, MUP, 1932. 78p. (ACER Educational Research Series, no 12). Contents: The child in the family by M. Lush; The child at school by J. McRae; The child and the community by J. T. Lawton; The importance of habit by N. A. Albiston; The growth of character by L. J. Wrigley.

1934 (936) BRIDGE, M. The effect on retention of different methods of revision. Melb, MUP, 1934. 55p. (ACER Educational Research Series, no 28).

(937) WHEELER, D. K. The value of the prevention of error as a teaching device. Melb, MUP, 1934. 31p. (ACER Educational Research Series, no 30).

1936 (938) HILL, M. Training to reason; an investigation into the possibility of training in seeing relations in evidence. Melb, MUP, 1936. 71p. (ACER Educational Research Series, no 44).

1937 (939) THOMAS, M. E. The efficacy of broadcasts to schools and classroom lessons. Melb, MUP, 1937. 48p. (ACER Educational Research Series, no 48).

(940) VICTORIAN Teachers Union. The case for small classes; an appeal to the intelligent elector. Melb, 1937. 4p.

1938 (941) GRIFFITHS, M. M. The relative efficiency of part and whole methods of presentation in the development of concepts. Melb, MUP, 1938. 92p. (ACER Educational Research Series, no 52).

1940 (942) LAW, A. J. Modern teaching. Melb, R & M, 1940. 149p. New revised edition 1949.

1944 (943) COOK, P. H. The theory and technique of child guidance. Melb, MUP for ACER, 1944. 136p.

1945 (944) BALLINA School of Method, Ballina, NSW October 1945. Education to meet the needs of a community. [Murwillumbah, NSW, 1945?]. 118p.

(945) ROSENTHAL, N. H. Films in instruction: Part 1. Films - their use and misuse. Part 2. The teachers manual. Melb, R & M, 1945. 2 vols.

(946) SOUTH Australian Public Teachers Union. Jubilee celebrations, 1895-1945. Adel, The Union, 1945. 8p.

1947 (947) CUNNINGHAM, K. S. and Morey, E. A. Children need teachers: a study of the supply and recruitment of teachers in Australia and overseas. Melb, MUP for the ACER, 1947. (ACER Educational Research Series, no 62).

(948) THE MARRIED woman teacher and the right to teach. Melb, ACER, 1947. 3 leaves. (Information Bulletin, no 7). 'Reproduced in slightly abbreviated form from Press Communication no 196/R1391 of the International Bureau of Education, Geneva, dated December, 1946'.

1948 (949) LAW, A. J. Modern teaching. Melb, R & M, 1948. 149p.

1949 (950) COOLING, G. C. Here's a villain. Brisb, Watson Ferguson, 1949. 254p. Anecdotes about author's career as a teacher.

1955 (951) BLAKEMORE, G. L. Individualising education in the elementary school. Wagga Wagga, NSW Daily Advertiser, 1955. 95p.

(952) OESER, O. A. , editor. Teacher, pupil and task; elements of social psychology applied to education: a practical manual for teachers. Lond, Tavistock, 1955. 209p.

1959 (953) DUFF, T. S. Classroom practices and child development; an enquiry into the judgements of certain groups concerned with education on the benefits to the child of specified classroom practices. Melb, ACER, 1959. 70p.

1960 (954) PHILLIPS, W. Mental health; is it a teacher's problem?
Melb, Vic Inst of Educational Research Primary Education Today
Group, [1960?]. (VIER Educational Pamphlet, no 2).

1961 (955) HAINE, H. E. Classroom psychology. Brisb, Jacaranda, 1961.
362p.

(956) MADDERN, I. T. Discipline and class control. Melb, Vic
Secondary Teachers Assn, 1961. 24p. (Education Series, no 2).

1962 (957) KEEVES, J. P., compiler. Notes on learning and programmed
instruction. Melb, ACER, [1962?] 11 leaves.

(958) KEEVES, J. P. A review of programmed instruction. Melb,
ACER, 1962. 109p.

(959) WYNDHAM, H. S. The search for better schools. [Syd,
the Author, 1962?]. 13p.

1963 (960) FOSTER, G. A report on closed-circuit television teaching
experiment at G. V. Brooks High School, Launceston, Tasmania.
Launceston, the School, 1963. 53p.

(961) KEEVES, J. P. A report on certain new educational materials.
Hawthorn, Vic, ACER, 1963. 61 leaves. (Special Distribution
Report, no 4).

(962) VICTORIAN Secondary Teachers Association. The Teachers
Tribunal. Melb, 1963. 15p.

1964 (963) BASSETT, G. W. Each one is different: teaching for individual
differences in the primary school; a contribution to the individual
education of Australian children, arising from a conference convened
by ACER in August 1962. Melb, ACER, 1964. 153p.

(964) AUSTRALIAN Broadcasting Control Board. Programme
Services Division. Bibliography of selected literature on educational
television. Melb, 1964. 11p.

(965) BELLHOUSE, A. R. Classroom teaching and discipline. Syd,
Wentworth, 1964. 66p.

(966) DAVIS, F. H. Report from Bangkok; a report on the World
Confederation of Organisations of the Teaching Profession's Asian
Regional Conference held at Bangkok in February 1964. Adel,
SA Inst of Teachers, 1964. 11p.

(967) HARRIS, J. The use of television in schools; a report.
[Melb, Vic Teachers Union?, 1964]. 38p.

(968) KEEVES, J. P. Evaluation report on use of two courses
of programmed instruction. Hawthorn, Vic, ACER, 1964. 1 vol
(various pagination).

1965 (969) AUSTRALIAN Broadcasting Commission. Educational television in developing countries; a report of an on-the-spot survey.
Syd, ABC and Nippon Hoso Kyokai, Japan, 1965. 120p.

(970) AUSTRALIAN College of Education. Each to his full stature.
Melb, Cheshire for the College, 1965. 135p.
Papers presented at the sixth annual conference of the Australian
College of Education, Brisbane, 1965.
Contents: Presidential address by H. S. Wyndham; The organisation
of schools for individual talent by R. W. McCulloch; Problems of
assessment in a system catering for individual talent by S. S. Dunn;
Full stature for the underprivileged by R. Adam; The conference
theme in retrospect by G. W. Bassett; The role of the student
counsellor by N. M. Niemann; The contribution of art education
to total development by H. White; Individual differences and
aboriginal education by B. A. Watts; 'Handicapped children' by M. E.
Thomas.

(971) FOSTER, G. Television; another aid for teachers. Hobart,
Education Dept, 1965. 66p.

(972) KEEVES, J. P. Programmed instruction in Australia, 1965.
Hawthorn, Vic, ACER, 1965. 8p. (Information Bulletin, no 44).

1966 (973) AUSTRALIAN College of Education. Teachers in Australia;
an appraisal. Melb, Cheshire for the College, 1966. 208p.
Contents: Some problems in educational policy in democratic
societies by P. H. Partridge (The 1966 Buntine Oration); What
the statistical survey reveals by G. F. Berkeley; Teacher education
in the Martin Report by W. E. C. Andersen; The professionalization
of the student teacher by H. B. Lindsay; Desirable training of teachers
by H. Menzies-Smith; From secondary student to secondary teacher
by A. W. Jones; Teacher education in England by J. A. Richardson;
Training of technical teachers by L. R. Fragar; School counselling
in NSW by I. M. V. James; Patterns of art and craft teacher training by M. E. Scott.

(974) QUEENSLAND. Department of Education. Research and
Curriculum Branch. An evaluation of a non-graded organisation
in a large Queensland Primary school. Brisb, 1966. 31 leaves.
(Bulletin no 31).

1967 (975) AUSTIN, R. and others. An empirical evaluation of tutorials
in a first-year university subject. Kensington, NSW, Educational
Research Unit University of NSW, 1967. 15p. (Occasional
Publication, no 4).

(976) AUSTRALIAN College of Education. Teachers in Australian
schools; a report. Melb, 1967. 151p.

(977) BASSETT, G. W. , editor. Teaching in the primary school.
Syd, Novak, 1967. 343p. (Teaching Methods Series, vol 2).
'This book is devoted to considering the way in which the primary
school curriculum may be taught' (preface).

(978) HARLEY, B. , and others. A synthesis of teaching methods.
Australian ed. Syd, McGraw-Hill, 1967. 238p.

(979) MODERN Teaching Methods Association. Digest of modern teaching. Melb, 1967. 80p.

(980) SEMINAR for Committee Members of Subject Associations, Melbourne, 1967. Report. Melb, Vic Commercial Teachers Assn [1967?] . 27p.
Seminar organised by Joint Council of Subject Associations of Victoria.

1968 (981) ACT Teachers Association. Results of a survey on teaching conditions in the ACT as at 31 July 1968. Canb, 1968. 8 leaves.

(982) DE LA SALLE College, Malvern, Vic. A report on CCTV in a high school using a video tape recorder. Malvern, Vic, 1968. 22 leaves.

(983) DUNKIN, M. J. The nature and resolution of role conflicts among Queensland primary school teachers; an application of field theory. St Lucia, Qld. , Univ of Qld Press, 1968. 27p. (Queensland University Faculty of Education Papers, vol 1, no 1).

(984) MACKIE, M. Educative teaching. Syd, A & R, 1968. 297p.

(985) NEW South Wales Teachers Federation. Chronicle II of the Associate, 1918-68; 50 years of educational progress. Sans Souci, NSW, 1968. 7p.

(986) RICHARDSON, P. and Van der Veur, K. Teachers in the urban community. Canb, New Guinea Research Unit, ANU, 1968. 72p. (Australian National University, Canberra. New Guinea Research Unit. Bulletin no 21).

(987) SURETIES, B. , Penniceard, C. and Shelton, J. A point of understanding; creative writing in some fourth year classes. Melb, Cassell Aust, 1968. 95p. (Studies in Education, no 1).
'A record of imaginative writing by children in carefully observed circumstances on a limited number of occasions'.

(988) WYKES, O. and King, M. G. Teaching of foreign languages in Australia. Hawthorn, Vic, ACER, 1968. 182p. (Educational Research Series, no 84).

1969 (989) HARLEY, B. and Randall, G. C., editors. Background to teaching. Syd, McGraw-Hill, 1969. 221p.
'This book is designed to help students and teachers by presenting a collection of recent points of view on topics immediately relevant to teaching and school administration' (preface).

(990) HAWKINS, B. Television in the Australian classroom. Hawthorn, Vic, ACER, 1969. 53p. (Quarterly Review of Australian Education, vol 3, no 1).

(991) INFANT Mistresses Seminar, Frankston Teachers College, 1969. Educational leadership. Melb, Education Dept, 1969. 1 vol (various pagination).

(992) NEW South Wales. Department of Education. Public Relations Office. School of the Air. Syd, Govt Pr, 1969. 17p.

(993) PAPUA New Guinea. Department of Education. Teaching in Papua and New Guinea, Canb, Dept of External Territories, [1969?]. 26p.

(994) SEMINAR on the Role of the Computer in the Secondary School, Adelaide, 1969. Proceedings, edited by B.W. Smith. Canb, Aust Computer Society, 1969. 250p.

(995) SPAULL, A. A preliminary survey of the state school teachers organisations in Australia. Clayton, Vic, Faculty of Education Monash Univ, 1969. 39 leaves.

(996) TEACHERS and national service, December 1969. Melb, 1969. 45p.
Written by Victorian Secondary Teachers Association, Victorian Teachers Union, Technical Teachers Association of Victoria. Published in co-operation with the Department of Labour and National Service and the Education Department of Victoria.

(997) TRAVERS, B.H. The profession of school-mastering; the Chairman's address to the NSW Chapter, Australian College of Education, 1969. [Syd, 1969?]. 15p.

(998) VICTORIA. Audio-Visual Education Centre. Audio-visual teaching materials for commercial subjects. Melb, 1969. 40p.

1970 (999) ANDERS, D.J. Report on teacher recruitment campaign conducted in Britain and North America, November 1969 to February 1970. Adel, Education Dept of SA, [1970?]. 1 vol (various pagination).

(1000) AUSTRALIAN Broadcasting Commission. Using radio and television in the classroom; a guide to classroom practice. Syd, 1970. 15p.

(1001) BARKER, L.J. and others. The development of a low cost teaching carrel. Toowoomba, Qld Inst of Technology, Darling Downs, 1970. 32p.
Research project report to the Commonwealth Advisory Committee on Advanced Education.

(1002) CAMPBELL, W.J., editor. Scholars in context; the effects of environments on learning. Syd, Wiley, 1970. 429p.
'This book aims to explore the nature, and effects upon school learning, of environments varying from nation to classroom' (preface).

(1003) DOENAU, S.J. Sit still, listen and be quiet. Epping, NSW, K.J. Wass, 1970. 132p.

(1004) HAWKINS, B. Closed curcuit television in teachers colleges. Hawthorn, Vic, ACER, 1970. 39p. (Occasional Paper, no 3).

(1005) HUTTON, M.A. and Ellison, A. Some aspects of pictorial perception among Niuginians. Konedobu, Psychological Services Section Department of the Public Service Board, Territory of Papua and New Guinea, 1970. 14p. (Research Report, no 1).

(1006) MACKIE, M. and Kelly, G. What is right? Case studies in the ethics of education. Syd, A & R, 1970. 147p.

(1007) NEW South Wales. Department of Education. Teaching with the New South Wales Department of Education. Syd, 1970. 16p.

(1008) PAPUA New Guinea Teachers Association. Report on the teachers conference held at Port Moresby Teachers College, December 1970. Boroko, Papua, [1971?]. 58 leaves.

(1009) QUEENSLAND. Department of Education. Queensland's schools of the air. Brisb, 1970. 16p.

(1010) SPAULL, A.D. A report of the Technical Teachers Association of Victoria education campaign during the state elections 1970. Clayton, Vic, Monash Univ, Faculty of Education, 1970. 21 leaves.

1971 (1011) AUSTRALIAN Unesco Seminar, Melbourne, 1970. Developing in schools a critical study of film and television, and Report to Director General of Unesco by A.W. Hodginson. Canb, Aust Govt Publishing Service for Aust Advisory Committee for Unesco, 1971. 121p.

(1012) COVERDALE, G.M. Teacher morale; a pilot study. Syd, School of Education, Macquarie Univ, 1971. 56p.

(1013) DAVIES, A.T. and Duke, C., editors. The retention of teachers; papers prepared for a seminar arranged by the Centre for Continuing Education, October 27-29 1971. Canb, ANU, 1971. 74p.

(1014) FISHER, G.A. 'So grows the tree ...', being an auto-biographical miscellany. Armidale, NSW, the Author, [1971]. 177p.

(1015) GREY, A. The perceptive teacher; a compilation of seven essays on aspects of perception with discussion points for teachers and parents. Singleton, NSW, the Author, 1971. 130p.

(1016) NEW South Wales Institute of Inspectors of Schools. The inspectors look at inspection. Wahroonga, NSW, 1971. 8p.

(1017) NEW South Wales Teachers Federation. The retention of teachers; submission to the ANU Centre for Continuing Education Seminar, October 1971. Syd, 1971. 7 leaves.

(1018) ROE, E. Some dilemmas of teaching. Melb, OUP, 1971. 183p.

(1019) SEMINAR on Educational Administration, Centre for Continuing Education, Wangaratta, Victoria, 1970. Educational administration series 2 no 1; the principal and school climate; proceedings of a seminar for principals and senior teachers, March 24-26, 1971. Wangaratta, Vic, the Centre, 1971. 106p.

(1020) SUMNER, B. J. A study of teacher resignations in South Australia. Adel, Education Dept, 1971. 24p.

(1021) TURNER, J. L. , Oglesby, G. S. and Lindsay, B. A. The Nathalia scheme. Shepparton, Vic, Waterwheel Press, 1971. 124p.

(1022) VICTORIAN Secondary Teachers Association. Professional action '71. Melb, 1971. 12p.

1972 (1023) AUSTRALIAN Broadcasting Commission. 'Sesame Street'; an ABC Research Interim Report. [Syd, 1972?]. 8 leaves.

(1024) AUSTRALIAN Teachers Federation and Victorian Teachers Union. Make your vote count for education: VTU election kit. Melb, 1972. 22 leaves.

(1025) BESSANT, B. and Spaull, A. D. Teachers in conflict. Melb, MUP, 1972. 107p. (The Second Century in Australian Education, no 3).

(1026) GILCHRIST, M. The psychology of creativity. Melb, MUP, 1972. 101p. (Second Century in Australian Education series, no 4).

(1027) GOSLING, G. W. H. Telecommunications in education; a report commissioned by the Australian Post Office on uses and planned uses by Australian educators of telecommunications facilities. Hawthorn, Vic, ACER, 1972. 120p.

(1028) MORRIS, W. C. Arches of time; memoirs. Hobart, A. Morris, 1972. 180p.

(1029) TEACHERS and national service, 1972. Published by the Victorian Secondary Teachers Association, Victorian Teachers Union and Technical Teachers Association of Victoria in co-operation with the Department of Education and Science, Department of Labour and National Service, Education Department of Victoria and State Superannuation Board. Melb, 1972. 42p.

(1030) VICTORIAN Council of School Organisations. Consolidated statement of policy adopted by ... conferences ... 1964-70; with addenda, 1971. Melb, 1972. 2 vols.

(1031) VICTORIA. Education Department. Communication and the principal, a pivotal role: [papers from a seminar of primary principals, Somers, August 1972]. Melb, 1972. 98p.

(1032) VICTORIA. Education Department. Curriculum and Research Branch. Curriculum evaluation; a possible approach, by G. P. White. Melb, 1972. 23p. (Occasional Paper, no 3).

(1033) VICTORIA. Education Department. Curriculum and Research Branch. What skills? by R. Cleaves. Melb, 1972. 23p. (Occasional Paper no 2).

(1070) FRASER, I.C. Review of the evaluation of listening skills. Melb, ACER, 1962. 12 leaves.

(1071) PAPPAS, G.S. Reading in the primary school. Melb, Macmillan, 1962. 241p.
Chapter 10 on 'Remedial reading' by M. Kemp; Chapter 13 on 'School libraries and the reading program' by B. Thompson.

(1072) SPEARRITT, D. Listening comprehension; a factorial analysis. Melb, ACER, 1962. 159p. (Educational Research Series, no 76).

(1073) ANDREWS, R.J. The reading attainments of primary school children in three Queensland schools. St Lucia, Qld, 1964. (Queensland Papers. Faculty of Education. Papers, vol 1, no4).

(1074) BANNAN, E.M., Harris, D.A., McLeod, J., Radford, W.C. and Sommerville, B.D. Aspects of reading in the primary school; a review of research. Melb, ACER, 1964. 141p.
Contents: Oculo-motor habits and their improvements by W.C. Radford; Readiness for reading by B.D. Sommerville; Aspects of teaching by D.A. Harris; Errors in reading and obtaining meaning by J. McLeod; Format by E.M. Bannan; Research conducted by Australia into reading and its problems by W.C. Radford.

(1075) HIGGINS, F. Music education in the primary school. Melb, Macmillan, 1964. 184p.

(1076) RUSSELL, D.H. and Russell, E.F. Listening aids through the grades; one hundred and ninety listening activities. Melb, ACER, 1964. 109p.
'Adapted and reprinted for distribution in Australia by permission of the original publisher, the Bureau of Publications, Teachers College, Columbia University, New York, USA'.

(1077) BOLT, D. and Wrigley, D.F. Education through environment written ... as the Canberra project for the first Assembly of the Australian Society for Education through Art held in Canberra, May 1965. Canb, Aust Society for Education through Art, 1965. 18p.

(1078) HORNER, V. Music education; the background of research and opinion. Hawthorn, Vic, ACER, 1954. 232p. (Educational Research Series, no 79).
Second part of this survey, by G. Bartle, published in 1968, entry 1100

(1079) HUNT, H.A.K. and Keeves, J.P. Dependent clauses in Latin; an exploratory study of the value of programmed instruction. Hawthorn, Vic, ACER, 1965. 20 leaves. (Research Bulletin, no 1).

(1034) VICTORIAN Teachers Union. Proposed bill for the establishment of a Victoria Institute of Teacher Education. Melb, 1972. 24 leaves.
Prepared in co-operation with the Council of Teachers Colleges Staff Associations (Victoria) and the Victorian Association of Principals of Teachers Colleges.

(ii) Subject Teaching

Works in this section are devoted to particular aspects of subject teaching. Text books have not been included.

(a) Humanities

Includes art, language and literature, reading, listening, spelling.

1932 (1035) GRIFFITHS, D.C. The psychology of literary appreciation; a study in psychology and education. Melb, MUP, 1932. 142p. (ACER Educational Research Series, no 13).

(1036) PARKER, H.T. Defects of speech in school children; results of an investigation made in the Tasmanian state schools. Melb, MUP, 1932. 96p. (ACER Educational Research Series, no 15).

1933 (1037) BIAGGINI, E.G. English in Australia; taste and training in a modern community. Melb, MUP, 1933. 134p. (ACER Educational Research Series, no 19).

1939 (1038) AUSTRALIAN Council for Educational Research. Committee on the Teaching of Modern Languages in the Secondary School. Modern languages in the secondary school. Melb, MUP, 1939. 30p.

1948 (1039) HARDIE, C.D. A minimum vocabulary. Melb, ACER, 1948. 20p.

(1040) HUNT, H.A.K. Training through Latin. Melb, MUP for the ACER, 1948. 186p.

1949 (1041) AUSTRALIAN Council for Educational Research. Report on aspects of arithmetic and English in Australian schools; curriculum survey. Melb, 1949. 1 vol (various pagination).

1950 (1042) AUSTRALIAN Council for Educational Research. Curriculum survey; summary report to the directors of education. Melb, 1950. 1 vol (various pagination).

1951 (1043) AUSTRALIAN Council for Educational Research. English and arithmetic for the Australian child. Melb, 1951. 36p.
'It presents a selection of facts from a comprehensive survey of courses of study and teaching practices, and from the results of tests ... and offers occasional comment' (foreword).

(1044) COOPER, C.G. Classics in modern education. Brisb, Univ of Qld Press, 1951. 16p. (University of Queensland Papers. Faculty of Arts. vol 1, no 1).

(1045) ERRORS in the use of English by a group of preschool
children. Melb, ACER, 1951. 8 leaves. (Information Bulletin,
no 22).

(1046) PRONUNCIATION errors in the spontaneous speech of a
group of preschool children. Melb, ACER, 1951. 6 leaves.
(Information Bulletin, no 21).

(1047) RUSSELL, D. H. and Karp, E. E. Reading aids through
the grades; three hundred developmental reading activities.
Melb, ACER, 1951. 124p.
Australian edition, with some changes in spelling and phraseology
of the second edition published by Teachers College, Columbia
University, USA.

(1048) A SPEECH vocabulary of Australian preschool children.
Melb, ACER, 1951. 9 leaves. (Information Bulletin, no 23).

(1049) THE STRUCTURE of the spontaneous speech of a group
of preschool children. Melb, ACER, 1951. 8 leaves. (Information
Bulletin, no 24).

1952 (1050) GROWTH in vocabulary and expression in the first twelve
months at school. Melb, ACER, 1952. 14 leaves. (Information
Bulletin, no 25).

(1051) QUEENSLAND. Department of Public Instruction. Research
and Guidance Branch. Research findings on spelling. Brisb, 1952.
13 leaves. (Bulletin no 6).

1953 (1052) RADFORD, W. C. The functional classification of child
speech. Melb, ACER, 1953. 20 leaves. (Information Bulletin,
no 30).

(1053) RADFORD, W. C. Growth in vocabulary and expression in
the first two years at school; a pilot investigation. Melb, ACER,
1953. 14 leaves. (Information Bulletin, no 29).

1954 (1054) RADFORD, W. C. Socio-economic status and English
expression. Melb, ACER, 1954. 14 leaves. (Information Bulletin,
no 33).

(1055) STRANG, R. and others. Study type of reading exercises.
Melb, ACER, 1954. 100p.
Australian edition, with several minor changes in the text, of the
1935 edition printed by Teachers College, Columbia University,
USA. A teachers manual, 'Improvement of reading in secondary
school', was also issued.

1955 (1056) MELBOURNE Teachers College Seminar for Secondary and
Technical School Teachers, 1955. Report of the art groups.
Melb, Melb Teachers College, 1955. 1 vol (various pagination).

(1057) QUEENSLAND. Department of Public Instru
and Guidance Branch. An investigation of methods
reading in infants schools. Brisb, 1955. 49 leaves
no 9).

1956 (1058) QUEENSLAND. Department of Public Instru
and Guidance Branch. Research findings in reading
17 leaves. (Bulletin no 10).

1958 (1059) DIMMACK, M. Modern art education in the
Melb, Macmillan, 1958. 164p.

(1060) QUEENSLAND. Department of Public Instru
and Guidance Branch. Reading methods for Queens
schools. Brisb, 1958. 47 leaves. (Bulletin no 17)

(1061) QUEENSLAND. Department of Public Instru
and Guidance Brnach. Studies in spelling. Brisb,
(Bulletin no 16).

1959 (1062) HORNER, A. M. Good speech in the making
and methods of speech education for the junior scho
Rigby, 1959. 124p.

(1063) RICHARDSON, J. A. and Hart, J. A. Books
reader; a teacher's guide to books for backward ch
ACER, 1959. 74p.
2nd edition, 1961; 3rd edition 1966; 4th edition 19

1960 (1064) AUSTRALIAN Unesco Seminar on Drama in
Teachers College, 16-22 August 1958. Report. Sy
Advisory Committee for Unesco, 1960. 120p.

(1065) INSTITUTE of Inspectors of Schools of New
Suggestions for the teaching of reading in upper pri
edited by A. W. Stacey. Rockdale, NSW, Atlantic,

(1066) QUEENSLAND. Department of Education.
Guidance Branch. Two studies in reading. Brisb,
(Bulletin no 21).
Contents: Part 1. A comparison of present and pa
standards in Grave V; Part 2. A reading improve
in three Brisbane High schools.

(1067) RADFORD, W. C. A word list for Australia
suggestions for its use. Melb, ACER, 1960. 2 vo
Contents: vol 1, Student edition; vol 2, Teachers

1961 (1068) DERHAM, F. Art for the child under seven
Preschool Assn, 1961. 52p.
Second edition 1962; third edition 1967.

(1069) PITTMAN, G. A. Report on the teaching of
Territory of Papua and New Guinea. Port Moresby
1961. 43p.

(1080) NEW South Wales. University. Drama at the University of New South Wales; the Department of Drama, the National Institute of Dramatic Art, the Old Tote Theatre Company, the University of New South Wales Drama Foundation. Syd, 1965. 20p.

(1081) QUEENSLAND. Department of Education. Research and Curriculum Branch. Studies in primary school reading. Brisb, [1965?]. 18 leaves. (Bulletin no 28).

1966 (1082) AUSTRALIAN Association of Adult Education. Language teaching for adult education; papers from the workshop for adult education language tutors held by Monash University, 1965. Melb, 1966. 57p.

(1083) AUSTRALIAN National Advisory Committee for Unesco. Australian Unesco seminar on school music, Syd, May 1965. [Syd, 1966]. 313p.

(1084) BENNETT, D. M. SRA Writing Skills Laboratory, Part 1. Evaluation report. Hawthorn, Vic, ACER, 1966. 31p. (Information Bulletin, no 48).

(1085) GOODENOUGH, W. W. A report on the range and nature of research into the teaching of English in Australia. Syd, Aust Assn for the Teaching of English, 1966. 8p.

(1086) GOSLING, G. W. H. Marking English compositions. Hawthorn, Vic, ACER, 1966. 103p. (Educational Research Series, no 81).

(1087) NICKSON, N. J. Education through music; two lectures delivered at the University of Queensland in 1966. St Lucia, Qld, Univ of Qld Press, 1967. 35p. (Queensland University Inaugural Lectures).

(1088) WYKES, O. Survey of foreign language teaching in the Australian universities; a report prepared by Olive Wykes with recommendations by the Sub Committee on Foreign Languages. Canb, Aust Humanities Research Council, 1966. 53p.

1967 (1089) ANDERSON, J. A scale to measure the reading difficulty of children's books. St Lucia, Qld, Univ of Qld Press, 1967. 21p. (Queensland. University. Faculty of Education. Papers, vol 1, no 6).

(1090) AUSTRALIAN Society for Education Through Art. Art education bibliography; a list of books concerned with the theories and philosophies of art education. Adel, 1967. 47p.

(1091) AUSTRALIAN Society for Education Through Art. Investigating child art competitions. [Brisb?], 1967. 28p.

(1092) AUSTRALIAN Society for Education Through Art. Report on art teacher training. [Syd?], 1967. 16p.
The last named three works were produced in NSW for the Second Biennial Assembly of the Australian Society for Education Through Art.

(1093) BENNETT, D. M. New methods and materials in spelling; a critical analysis. Hawthorn, Vic, ACER, 1967. 160p. (Educational Research Series, no 82).

(1094) JOYNT, D. and Cambourne, B. The development of the regulatory role of speech in Australian children. Armidale, NSW, University of New England, Dept of Education, [1967?]. 37p. (New England Papers on Education, no 1).

(1095) LAMERAND, R. J. A bibliography on teaching and testing in foreign languages, with special reference to programmed learning. Melb, ACER, 1967. 1 vol (unpaged).

(1096) POSTGRADUATE studies in the humanities in Australia; three essays by Sir Keith Hancock, P. H. Partridge and R. W. V. Elliott. Syd, Syd Univ Press for the Aust Humanities Research Council, 1967. 36p. (AHRC Occasional Paper, no 11).

(1097) QUEENSLAND. Department of Education. Research and Curriculum Branch. Evaluation of a writing skills laboratory in a Queensland state high school. Brisb, 1967. 36 leaves. (Bulletin no 32).

(1098) SCHOENHEIMER, H. P. , editor. Education through English; some aspects of the learning and teaching of English. Melb, Cheshire, 1967. 273p.

1968 (1099) ANDERSON, A. W. Speed up your reading; a course for improving reading efficiency designed and standardised in conjunction with the Adult Education Board of the University of Western Australia. 2nd ed. Nedlands, WA, Univ of WA Press, 1968. 208p.

(1100) BARTLE, G. Music in Australian schools. Hawthorn, Vic, ACER, 1968. 298p. (Educational Research Series, no 83). 'Second part of a survey of music education in schools ... The first part was a survey of the research and related later literature made by Mr V. Horner and published in 1965' (foreword). See entry 1078.

(1101) BURKE, D. T. On dyslexia; case for spelling reform with historical and economic considerations. Adel, Aust New Transcrybd Speech, [1968?]. 14 leaves.

(1102) HARRISON, R. N. and Hooper, F. , editors. Dyslexia symposium. Melb, Aust College of Speech Therapists, [1968?]. 232p.

(1103) MOORE, W. E. The effects of SRA laboratory usage with fifth grade children. Syd, Dept of Education, Division of Research and Planning, 1968. 39p. (Technical Report Research Bulletin, no 29).

(1104) QUEENSLAND. Department of Education. Research and Curriculum Branch. Psycholinguistic research in Queensland schools, 1961-66, prepared in collaboration with N. W. M. Hart. Brisb, 1968. 92p. (Bulletin no 34).

1969 (1105) MALING, J. Using an aural stimulus for a writing task; a report on the writing produced in response to a nationwide experimental broadcast on 1 August 1968. Hawthorn, Vic, ACER, 1969. 35p. (Occasional Paper no 1).

(1106) QUEENSLAND. Department of Education. Research and Curriculum Branch. Standards of achievement in reading, spelling and certain study skills, Queensland Grade 7 pupils. Brisb, 1969. 31p. (Bulletin no 36).

(1107) THE TEACHING of Asian languages and studies in schools; proceedings of a seminar held at Glenn College, La Trobe University, Saturday 26 July 1969, edited by W. H. Martell. Melb, Australia-India Society of Vic, 1969. 64p.

1970 (1108) AUSTRALIAN Unesco Seminar, National Gallery of Victoria, 1967. Professional training of the artist. Canb, Aust National Advisory Committee for Unesco, 1970. 81p.

(1109) HUXLEY, D. R. The listening ability of students at tertiary level. Newcastle, NSW, Newcastle Teachers College, [1970?]. 12p.

(1110) QUEENSLAND. Department of Education. Van Leer Project. Research report on some aspects of the language development of preschool children. Brisb, 1970. 101p.

(1111) RICHARDSON, D. Art films for teaching; a select and classified catalogue of 16mm films available in Australia. Canb, Aust National Advisory Committee for Unesco, 1970. 64p.

(1112) ROPER, T. W. and Waten, H. Differences in reading skills in a number of inner and outer suburban Melbourne high schools. Bundoora, Vic, Centre for the Study of Urban Education, School of Education, La Trobe Univ, [1970]. 22p.

(1113) VICTORIA. Education Department. Secondary English Committee. Teaching English in the secondary school; the collected papers of the Secondary English Committee 1970. Melb, 1970. 187p.

1971 (1114) ANDREWS, R. J., editor. Reading and the exceptional child; proceedings of a seminar, Fred and Eleanor Schonell Educational Research Centre, University of Queensland, May 1971. St Lucia, Qld, Univ of Qld, 1971. 101p.

(1115) DIRECTIONS in Australian secondary school English, edited by B. H. Bennett and J. A. Hay. Melb, Longman, 1971. 115p.

(1116) FLUX, W. R. A guide to the aims, philosophy and techniques of sequential reading in practice. Cheltenham, Vic, Standard Stationers, 1971. 30p.

(1117) HEPWORTH, T. S. Dyslexia; the problem of reading retardation. Syd, A & R, 1971. 100p.

(1118) HISTORY Teachers Association of New South Wales.
Transcript of history seminar day. [Syd], 1971. 1 vol (unpaged).

(1119) KEEPES, J. M. and Rechter, B. Report on higher school
certificate English expression. Hawthorn, Vic, ACER, 1971.
2 vols.

(1120) MARTIN, J. S. and Sjorberg, B., editors. The teaching
of Swedish in Melbourne; report on the teaching of Swedish in the
Department of Germanic Studies at the University of Melbourne.
Carlton, Vic, 1971. 64 leaves.

(1121) ROSEN, J. K. Comparative professional preparation for
speech pathology and audiology in English speaking countries.
Syd, the Author, 1971. 72 leaves.

(1122) VICTORIA. Education Department. Curriculum and
Research Branch. 'Breakthrough to Literacy'; a follow-up study
of reading performance in the second year of school, by M. Cullen.
Melb, 1971. 19p. (RR 1/71).

(1123) VICTORIA. Education Department. Curriculum and
Research Branch. Seriation and language; an examination of the
relationship between performance on seriation tasks and the development of relational length terms, by A. H. Walta. Melb, 1971.
21 leaves. (Research Report RR 7/71).

(1124) VICTORIA. Education Department. Remedial English
teaching in the secondary school; an introduction. Melb, 1971.
51p.
Prepared for the Standing Committee for English in Technical
Schools and the Curriculum and Research Branch.

(1125) YELLAND, H. T. The English teacher and creativity;
emotional development and the provision of activities. Nedlands,
WA, Secondary Teachers College, 1971. 8p. (Library Occasional
Paper, no 6).

1972 (1126) AUSTRALIAN reading education and research directory
1972, edited by G. S. and J. A. Johnson. Wagga Wagga, NSW,
Reading Centre, School of Teacher Education, Riverina College
of Advanced Education, 1972. 34p.

(1127) CURRICULUM Officers Conference on Primary Schools
English, Melbourne, 1971. Conference report to the Directors-
General of Education, compiled by W. T. Renehan with the assistance
of G. P. Withers and C. Vaughan. Hawthorn, Vic, ACER, 1972.
41p.
With supplement of conference papers. (unpaged).

(1128) HICKEY, D. Conceptual art; implications for art education
in the tertiary section. Preston, Vic, Preston Inst of Technology,
1972. 15 leaves.

(1129) JACKSON, M. S. Reading disability; experiment, innovation
and individual therapy. Syd, A & R, 1972. 79p.

(1130) NICHOLSON, T. A review of the Doman Delacato 'patterning' method. Adel, Research and Planning Branch Eudcation Dept, 1972 1 vol (various pagination).

(1131) QUEENSLAND. Department of Education. Research and Curriculum Branch. Improving reading through an oral language program. Brisb, 1972. 16p.

(1132) SCHOENHEIMER, H. P. , editor. English in Australian secondary schools. Melb, Cheshire, 1972. 174p.

(1133) VICTORIA. Education Department. Primary Schools English Committee. Overview English 1972. Melb, 1972. 3 leaves (Circular EP/6).

(b) Social Sciences

Includes civics, history, moral and physical education, social studies.

1930 (1134) CURREY, C. H. The study and teaching of history and civics Syd, Whitcombe & Tombs, 1930. 64p.

(1135) MORRIS, E. S. Physical education; an outline of its aims, scope, methods and organisation. Canb, Commonwealth Dept of Health, [193?] . 15p.

1934 (1136) HOY, A. , editor. Report on the teaching of history and civics in Victorian secondary schools, by a History Sub Committee of the Victorian Institute for Educational Research. Melb, MUP, 1934. 78p. (ACER Educational Research Series, no 23). Includes as Appendix A: Victorian secondary schools and education for international understanding by W. D. Forsyth.

1936 (1137) RAMSAY, A. H. and Johnson, M. Physical education in Victoria. Melb, ACER, 1936. 31p.

1939 (1138) SCHULZ, A. J. Character and its development. Adel, Hassell Press, 1939. 90p.

1941 (1139) McMAHON, J. T. Building character from within; the problem of leisure. Milwaukee, USA, Bruce Pub Co, 1941. 200p.

1945 (1140) LE MAISTRE, E. H. Physical education, Melb, OUP, 1945. 326p.

1947 (1141) KING, B. Sex education in New South Wales; [summary of a survey]. Melb, ACER, 1947. 4 leaves. (Information Bulletin, no 6).

(1142) SHANN, F. The Canberra system of school athletics; its approach, basis, organisation and results. Melb, MUP, 1947. 100p. (ACER Educational Research Series, no 63).

1951 (1143) CONNELL, W. F. New directions for character education. Melb, Character Education Enquiry, 1951. 8p. (Character Education, no 5).

(1144) CRUMP, M. Notes on character education in the home. Melb, Character Education Enquiry, 1951. 12p. (Character Education, no 6).

(1145) DUNLOP, E. W. Teaching social studies in the primary school. Armidale, NSW, Armidale Teachers College, 1951. 43p.

(1146) RAYNER, S. A. The special vocabulary of civics. Melb, MUP, 1951. 115p. (ACER Educational Research Series, no 65).

1952 (1147) CHARACTER Education Enquiry. Character education digest. Melb, 1952. 133p.

1956 (1148) WORLD Congress on Physical Education, University of Melbourne, 16-21 November 1956. Report. Melb, Aust Physical Education Assn, 1959. 178p.

1962 (1149) NEW South Wales. Department of Education. Physical Education Branch. A review of New South Wales national fitness and physical education activities, 1940-60. Syd, 1962. 11p.

1964 (1150) SWAIN, M. O. B. and Le Maistre, E. H. Fundamentals of physical education. Syd, Novak, 1964. 149p.

1967 (1151) BENNETT, D. M. and Piper, K. J. The present situation in, and the status of, the teaching of social sciences in Australian secondary schools. Part 1 and Part 1 continued. Melb, Australian National Advisory Committee for Unesco, 1967. 2 vols (National Seminar on the Teaching of the Social Sciences at the Secondary Level, Melbourne, 1967. Background Paper no 1).

(1152) HAINES, M. D. Social studies and teacher preparation. Adel, South Australian Institute of Teachers, [1967?] . 29p.

1968 (1153) BENNETT, D. M. The study of society in Australian schools. Hawthorn, Vic, ACER, 1968. 34p. (Quarterly Review of Australian Education, vol 2, no 1).

(1154) HISTORY Teachers Association, Newcastle, NSW. Senior history; Newcastle conference. Syd, Dept of Education, Inservice Training Branch, 1968. 65p.

1969 (1155) COATES, T. H. Some thoughts on moral education. Melb, Junior Schools Assn of Aust, 1969. 30p. (The Wells Oration, First, 1968).

(1156) PARTRIDGE, P. H. , Connell, W. F. and Cohen, S. W. Social science for the secondary school. Syd, Novak, 1969. 132p.

1970 (1157) DUFTY, D. G. , editor. Teaching about society; problems and possibilities. Adel, Rigby, 1970. 464p.

1971 (1158) BARCAN, A. Social science, history and the new curriculum. Syd, Hicks Smith, 1971. 136p.

(1159) BLACHFORD, K. The teaching of geography. Melb, Education Dept, 1971. 2 vols.

(1160) CONFERENCE on the Teaching of Sociology in Australia and New Zealand, Canberra 1970. [Papers], edited by J. Zubrzycki. Melb, Cheshire for the Sociological Assn of Aust and NZ, [1971]. 181p.

(1161) HUNT, F. J. and others. Social science and the school curriculum; a report on the Monash Project. Syd, A & R, 1971. 199p.

(1162) INTERNATIONAL Congress of the International Council on Health, Physical Education, and Recreation, 13th, Sydney, Australia July 13 - August 3 1970. [Papers]. Syd, 1971. 189p.

1972 (1163) FARLEY, P. E. and others. Teaching physical education in primary schools. Syd, McGraw Hill, 1972. 315p.

(1164) NEW South Wales. Department of Education. Statement of sex education policy. [Syd, 1972?]. 8 leaves.

(c) Sciences

Includes biology, chemistry, mathematics, physics.

1924 (1165) SYDNEY Teachers College Investigation Committee. Norms in the four fundamental operations of arithmetic. Syd, Dept of Education, 1924. 15p.
Second edition entitled 'Norms in Arithmetic', 1929.

1930 (1166) MIDDLETON, R. J. and Meldrum, H. J. The teaching of arithmetic. Syd, Teachers College Press, 1930. 111p.

1932 (1167) STANHOPE, R. W. The teaching of chemistry in the secondary schools of New South Wales, with special reference to the conditions existing in the United States of America. Melb, MUP, 1932. 74p. (ACER Educational Research Series, no 7).

1934 (1168) CUNNINGHAM, K. S. and Price, W. T. The standardisation of an Australian arithmetic test. Melb, MUP, 1934. 116p. (ACER Educational Research Series, no 21).

(1169) MELDRUM, H. J. An investigation into secondary school mathematics; an analysis of the results of Mathematics 1 Paper, Intermediate Certificate Examination, New South Wales, 1931. Melb, MUP, 1934. 19p. (ACER Educational Research Series, no 25).

1938 (1170) MITCHELL, F. W. The nature of mathematical thinking. Melb, MUP, 1938. 130p. (ACER Educational Research Series, no 53).

1940 (1171) AUSTRALIAN Council for Educational Research. Mathematics in the secondary school. Melb, MUP, 1940. 31p.
Contents: 1 Report of the Sub-Committee on the Teaching of Mathematics in Secondary School; 2 Mathematics as a training for reasoning by H. M. Campbell.

1949 (1172) AUSTRALIAN Council for Educational Research. Report on aspects of arithmetic and English in Australian Schools; curriculum survey. Melb, 1949. 1 vol (various pagination).

1950 (1173) AUSTRALIAN Council for Educational Research. Curriculum survey; summary report to the directors of education. Melb, 1950. 1 vol (various pagination).

(1174) PARKER, H. T. Achievement in formal arithmetic; a report on present achievement levels in primary grades together with suggestions for setting up grade standards. Hobart, Education Dept, 1950. 17 leaves.

1951 (1175) AUSTRALIAN Council for Educational Research. English and arithmetic for the Australian child. Melb, 1951. 36p.
'It presents a selection of facts from a comprehensive survey of courses of study and teaching practices, and from the results of tests ... and offers occasional comment' (foreword).

(1176) QUEENSLAND. Department of Public Instruction. Research and Guidance Branch. Research findings on some fundamental facts and processes in arithmetic. Brisb, 1951. 18 leaves. (Bulletin no 3).

1953 (1177) AUSTRALIAN Council for Educational Research. Courses of study, arithmetic, 1953; [collated to provide a comparative statement of age and grade locations up to age 12+]. Melb, 1953. 25 leaves.

(1178) QUEENSLAND. Department of Public Instruction. Research and Guidance Branch. Research findings in arithmetic. Brisb, 1953. 13 leaves. (Bulletin no 7).

1957 (1179) HARDIE, C. D., editor. Science in Australian primary schools. Melb, MUP, 1957. 97p.
Contents: The meaning of science and its place in education by C. S. Hardie; Aims and expected results of science teaching in the primary school by D. Merrilees; Science curricula in Australian primary schools by D. Merrilees; A suggested syllabus for primary school science by W. C. Radford; Apparatus and aids in the teaching of elementary science by F. J. Olsen; Teacher-training for primary school science by T. E. Doe; Educational measurement by means of scientifically constructed tests by F. J. Olsen; Topics for discussion and for future investigation by W. C. Radford.

1958 (1180) AUSTRALIAN Council for Educational Research. Provision for science teaching in the non government schools of Australia. Melb, ACER, 1958. 28p.

(1181) McMULLEN, A. Mathematics courses in US secondary schools. Melb ACER, 1958. 5 leaves. (Information Bulletin, no 37).
2nd Report (1958); 3rd Report (1959); 4th Report (1959); 5th Report (1959) published as ACER Information Bulletins 38, 39, 40 and 41).

1959 (1182) COVE, M. The place of science in the primary school
curriculum. Melb, Vic Inst of Educational Research Primary
Education Today Group, 1959. 9p. (Educational Pamphlet,
no 1).

1960 (1183) CLARK, M.L. Diagnostic testing in basic algebra; report
on a survey conducted in Victorian lower and middle secondary
grades. Melb, ACER, 1960. 22 leaves. (Special Distribution
Report, no 1).
Appendix of 27 leaves contains tables and graphs of errors.

1961 (1184) TURNER, M.L. and Dunn, S.S. ACER prematriculation
physics examination; report no 2. Melb, ACER, no 1961. 43
leaves.

1962 (1185) CLARK, M.L. Errors in arithmetical processes involving
fractions; a report on the results of diagnostic tests given to
Victorian pupils in primary school grade 6 and secondary school
form 1. Melb, ACER, 1962. 50p. (Special Distribution Report,
no 2).
Has a 27 page appendix of tables.

(1186) DODSON, H.L., compiler. Notes on mathematics in the
primary school. Melb, ACER. 1962. 42p.

(1187) KEEVES, J.P. New thinking in mathematics and contribution
of Dr. Z.P. Dienes. Melb, ACER, 1962. 5 leaves.

1963 (1188) BLAZELY, L.D. Diagnostic test in elementary mathematics.
Melb, ACER, 1963. 24 leaves. (Special Distribution Report, no 3).
Appendix of 28 leaves contains tables and graphs of errors.

(1189) FABENS, A.J. Some comments on the introductory mathematics curriculum in universities; a lecture delivered to the
Canberra Mathematical Association, May 1963. Canb, the Assn,
1963. 26p.

(1190) SHORT, L.N. and others. General biology, 1962; report
of a survey of student opinion concerning the content and teaching
of the subject [at the University of New South Wales]. Syd,
Univ of NSW Educational Research Unit, 1963. 47p.

1964 (1191) AUSTRALIA. Commonwealth Advisory Committee on Standards for Science Facilities in Independent Secondary Schools. The
design of science rooms. Canb, Prime Minister's Dept, 1964. 22p.
Second edition 1966.

(1192) CONFERENCE of Curriculum Officers of State Education
Departments, Melbourne, 1964. Primary school mathematics.
Hawthorn, Vic, ACER, 1964. 1 vol (various pagination).
The conference was convened by ACER at the request of the
Conference of Directors of Education.

(1193) NEW South Wales Teachers Federation. Science Committee. Preliminary requirements for the teaching of science in secondary schools, compiled ... in pursuance of decisions made by the 1964 High School Science Teachers Conference. Syd, 1964. 1 vol (various pagination).

(1194) KEEVES, J. P. Evaluation of achievement in mathematics; the tests used and attainment in mathematics of Australian pupils in the IEA Project, 1964. Hawthorn, Vic, ACER, 1966. 75p. (Memorandum Series, no 6).

(1195) SEMINAR on mathematics for twentieth century schools; proceedings of vacation seminar, Launceston, September 1963. Hobart, Govt Pr, 1964. 63p.

1965 (1196) BROWNELL, W. A. Arithmetic abstractions; the movement towards conceptual maturity under differing systems of instruction; a condensed version of the report of Co-operative Research Project no 1676. Melb, ACER, 1965. 55p.

(1197) KEEVES, J. P. Discovery and the development of mathematical concepts in the primary school. [Melb, ACER, 1965?]. 9p.

(1198) KEEVES, J. P. Some observations on mathematics in primary and lower secondary schools in England and the United States of America; a report on a recent visit. Hawthorn, Vic, ACER, 1965. 21 leaves. (Information Bulletin, no 43).

(1199) QUEENSLAND. Department of Education. Research and Guidance Branch. Studies in primary school mathematics. Brisb, 1965. 20 leaves. (Bulletin no 27).

(1200) RAWLINSON, R. W. An assessment of the Cuisenaire-Gattegno approach to the teaching of number in the first year at school. Melb, ACER, 1965. 73p. (Research Series, no 78).

(1201) TURNER, M. L. Evaluation and the new American science curricula. Hawthorn, Vic, ACER, 1965. 28p. (Information Bulletin, no 45).

(1202) AUSTRALIAN Council for Educational Research. Background in mathematics; a guide book to elementary mathematics for teachers in primary schools by J. P. Keeves and others. Melb, Education Dept of Vic & ACER, 1966. 287p.

(1203) DOWNES, L. W. and Paling, D. The teaching of arithmetic in tropical primary schools. Lond, OUP, 1966. 524p. (Unesco Handbooks on the Teaching of Science in Tropical Countries, vol 5).

(1204) MORISON, N. E. , Renehan, W. T. and Dunn S. S. Report on 1964 Victorian primary schools testing programme. Hawthorn, Vic, ACER, 1966. 44p. (Memorandum Series, no 5).

(1205) QUEENSLAND. Department of Education. Research and Curriculum Branch. An evaluation of achievements in and attitudes towards Grade 8 science in Queensland. Brisb, 1966. (Bulletin no 29).

(1206) QUEENSLAND. Department of Education. Research and Curriculum Branch. Experimental use of a programmed learning course in calculus at matriculation level. Brisb, 1966. 21 leaves. (Bulletin no 30).

1967 (1207) BIGGS, J. B. Mathematics and the conditions of learning; a study of arithmetic in the primary school by J. B. Biggs, with a statistical appendix by J. Hall. Slough, England, National Foundation for Educational Research in England and Wales, 1967. 452p. (Research Reports Second Series, no 2).

(1208) BUNKER, A. R. Understanding and teaching mathematics in the primary school. Syd, A & R, 1967. 180p.

(1209) CONNOR, D. V. Problem solving procedures in physics. Syd, Univ of NSW Educational Research Unit, 1967. 17p. (Occasional Publication, no 2).

(1210) INTERNATIONAL Association for the Evaluation of Educational Achievement (IEA). Science Project. Australian National Committee Science education in Australia; a statement. Hawthorn, Vic, ACER, 1967. 30 leaves.

(1211) QUEENSLAND. Department of Education. Research and Curriculum Branch. Prediction of success in matriculation and university mathematics. Brisb, 1967. 21 leaves. (Bulletin no 33).

(1212) RENEHAN, W. T. , Arney, D. J. and McBean, N. E. Report on 1965 Victorian primary schools testing programme. Hawthorn, Vic, ACER, 1967. 31p. (Memorandum Series, no 7).

1968 (1213) LUGG, D. Getting science across. Melb, Cheshire, 1968. 112p.

1969 (1214) ALEXANDER, A. E. Education and alchemy; the story of Wyndham science. Deniston, NSW, Secondary School Science Assn, 1969. 69p.

(1215) KEEVES, J. P. and Radford, W. C. Some aspects of performance in mathematics in Australian schools; a report on Australian participation in the International Study of Educational Achievement in Mathematics in 1964. Hawthorn, Vic, ACER, 1969. 83p. (Research Series no 85).

(1216) MESSEL, H. Wyndham science. Syd, Univ of Syd, 1969. 19p.

(1217) MESSEL, H. and Barker, E. N. The general philosophy behind the new integrated and co-ordinated science courses in NSW and the Science Foundation for Physics textbook series. [Syd, Science Foundation for Physics, Univ of Syd, 1969?]. 14p.

(1218) MEYER, G. R. A guide for pilot project study groups; Unesco pilot project on new approaches and techniques in biology teaching in Africa. [Paris?], Unesco, 1969. 66p.

1970 (1219) AUSTRALIAN Science Teachers Association. Conasta XVII, Melbourne 1968; proceedings. Melb, 1970. 127p.

(1220) AUSTRALIAN Science Education Project. Report of the Guidelines Conference, Monash University, January 1970. Melb, 1970. 40p.

(1221) COLLIS, K. F. Relationship between textbook orientation and mathematics achievement and attitude. St Lucia, Qld, Univ of Qld Press, 1970. 26p. (Queensland. University. Faculty of Education Papers, vol 1, no 8).

(1222) HODGKIN, C. G. Creativity and the advanced student. Nedlands, WA Secondary Teachers College, 1970. 3p. (STC Occasional Paper, no 3).

(1223) KELLY, V. Australian books for the science library; a bibliography for schools. Syd, School Library Assn of NSW, 1970. 76p.

(1224) MEYER, G. R. Two and one half months as consultant to the Government of Mauritius, Ministry of Education and Cultural Affairs on aspects of biology teaching, September to December 1969. [Paris], Unesco, 1970. 181p.

(1225) SCIENCE Summer School, Bendigo Teachers College, Victoria, 1970. Proceedings. Bendigo, Vic, the College, 1970. 82p.

(1226) TISHER, R. P. A study of verbal interaction in science classes and its association with pupils' understanding in science. St Lucia, Qld Univ Press, 1970. 35p. (University of Queensland, Faculty of Education Papers, vol 1, no 9).

(1227) WILSON, N. Objective tests and mathematical learning. Hawthorn, Vic, ACER, 1970. 130p.

1971 (1228) DEAN, I. A. Report on overseas agricultural education. Geelong Vic, Marcus Oldham Farm Agricultural College, 1971. 42p.

(1229) LEE DOW, K. C. Teaching science in Australian schools. Melb, MUP, 1971. 130p. (Second Century in Australian Education Series, no 1).

(1230) MACKAY, L. D. Understanding the nature of science among some secondary school students in Victoria. Clayton, Vic, Monash Univ Faculty of Education, 1971. 101p.

(1231) SOUTH Australia. Education Department. Research and Planning Branch. Evaluation of Primary Mathematics, Project 2, Reports 1, 2, 3. Adel, 1971. 3 vols.

1972 (1232) ARBIB, P. and Hanscomb, J. R. An audio-tutorial approach to physics. Syd, Tertiary Education Research Centre, Univ of NSW, 1972. 39p. (Monograph, no 3).

(1233) AUSTRALIAN Science Education Project. Position documents; a summary. Toorak, Vic, 1972. 7p.

(1234) RAMSEY, G. A. Curriculum development in secondary school science. Hawthorn, Vic, ACER, 1972. 2 vols (Quarterly Review of Australian Education vol 5 nos 1 & 2).

(1235) VICTORIA. Education Department. Curriculum and Research Branch. Primary Mathematics Curriculum Committee. Mathematics in the Primary School; introduction of metric units. Melb, 1972. 16p. (MP1/1972).

(1236) WESTERN Australian Tertiary Education Commission. Report on chemical engineering. Nedlands, WA, 1972. 30p.

(iii) Libraries in Education

Includes standards, education for librarianship, use of libraries in the educational process, but excludes general works on libraries.

1945 (1237) KIRBY, F. G. Libraries in secondary schools; a report on libraries in the secondary schools in Victoria, with suggestions for a post-war plan for school libraries. Melb, MUP, 1945. 48p.

1961 (1238) CUNNINGHAM, K. S. The Australian Council for Educational Research and library services in Australia. Melb, ACER, 1961. 31p.

(1239) HALLIDAY, W. A. The library in the secondary school; a handbook for the use of teachers and librarians. Melb, Halls Book Store, 1961. 119p.

1963 (1240) BROWN, A. M. Making books work; a course for the school library. Syd, Shakespeare Head, 1963. 119p.

(1241) DARLING, K. S. Using the library; a guide to library organisation. Melb, Cheshire, 1963. 36p.

(1242) LIBRARY Association of Australia. Childrens Libraries Section. Committee on Standards for Librarians of Childrens Libraries and for Library Work with Children. Libraries for children. Syd, 1963. 4p.

1964 (1243) ADVANCED Seminar on School and Children's Libraries. Melbourne, 1964. Report. Syd, Children's Libraries Section, Library Assn of Aust, 1964. 28p.

(1244) LIBRARY Association of Australia. Children's Libraries Section. Committee on School Libraries. A guide to minimum standards. Syd, 1964. 52p.

(1245) SMITH, C. E. How to find information in the library. Syd, Division of Research and Planning Dept of Education, 1964. 16p.

1965 (1246) BRYAN, H. Australian university libraries today and tomorrow. Syd, Bennett, 1965. 39p.

(1247) FENWICK, S. I. New trends in education and their impli-
cations for the school library, being the inaugural address of the
School Library Association of New South Wales, delivered on 30
July 1964 at Sydney Grammar School. Syd, School Library Assn
of NSW, 1965. 7p. (School Library Assn of NSW. Occasional
Papers, no 1).

(1248) LIBRARY Association of Australia. Public Libraries
Section. Victorian Division. Workshop, Hamilton, Vic, 1964;
education and the library. Papers. Melb, 1965. 65p.

(1249) McGRATH, L. H. Central library services of the education
departments of the Australian states. Adel, Libraries Board of
SA, 1965. 90p.

(1250) ROE, E. Teachers, librarians and children; a study of
libraries in education. Melb, Cheshire, 1965. 204p.

1966 (1251) FENWICK, S. I. School and children's libraries in Australia;
a report to the Children's Libraries Section of the Library Association
of Australia. Melb, Cheshire for the LAA, 1966. 36p.

(1252) FIELDING, F. D. O. Administrative organisation of Australian
university libraries. Adel, University and College Libraries Section
LAA, 1966. 1 vol (various pagination). (LAA. UCLS. News sheet.
Supplement no 1). Second edition 1971 (ANZ Book Co).

(1253) LIBRARY Association of Australia. Children's Libraries
Section. Committee on School Libraries. Standards and objectives
for school libraries; a guide to minimum standards and suitable
objectives prepared ... for the guidance of educational authorities,
teachers, librarians and parents. Melb, Cheshire for the LAA,
1966. 46p.

1967 (1254) BRYAN, H. Student preparation for using a university
library. Syd, School Library Assn of NSW, [1967?]. 15p.

(1255) CONFERENCE on School Libraries in South Australia,
Goolwa, 1967. Proceedings. Adel, Dept of Adult Education,
Univ of Adel, 1967. 70p. Conference arranged by Department
of Adult Education, University of Adelaide and the SA Branch of
the LAA.

(1256) FIELDING, F. D. O. Master of none; inaugural lecture
delivered at the University of Queensland, 16 March 1967. St Lucia,
Qld, Univ of Qld Press, 1968. 21p. (Queensland University Inaugural
Lectures).

(1257) HALL, N. The implementation of the Wyndham scheme and
its effect on school libraries. Syd, School Library Assn of NSW,
1967. 10p. (School Library Association of New South Wales.
Occasional Papers, no 2).

(1258) LIBRARY Association of Australia. The training of school librarians; report of the committee appointed by the Library Association of Australia. Syd, 1967. 31p.

(1259) SCHOOL Library Association of New South Wales. Council. Submission to the Director-General's Committee on School Libraries and Teacher Librarians. Syd, 1967. 7 leaves. (School Library Association of New South Wales. Occasional Papers, no 4).

(1260) STOCKDALE, N. and Graneek, J.J. The rationalization of library resources in Australia; two papers read before the tenth annual general meeting of the Australian Humanities Research Council on 4 November 1965. Syd, Syd Univ Press for the Council, 1967. 16p.

(1261) SUMPTER, V. The high school library in New South Wales under the Wyndham scheme. Syd, School Library Assn of NSW, 1967. 31p. (School Library Association of New South Wales. Occasional Papers, no 5).

1968 (1262) SCHOOL Library Association of North Queensland. The school library; proceedings of a seminar held at the University College of Townsville, 15 and 16 August 1967. Townsville, Qld, 1968. 83p.

(1263) TRASK, M. School libraries; a report to the nation. Melb, Cheshire for the Aust Library Week Council, 1968. 16p.

1969 (1264) AUSTRALIA. Secondary Schools Libraries Committee. Standards for secondary school libraries; preliminary statement, March 1969. Canb, Govt Pr, 1969. 24p. (Parliamentary Paper, no 39).

(1265) AUSTRALIA. Secondary Schools Libraries Committee; a preliminary statement. Canb, Govt Pr, 1969. 39p.

(1266) FIELDING, F.D.O. Why do schools require libraries? Townsville, Qld, School Library Assn of Qld, 1969. 10p. Address given to a seminar organised by the Queensland State Secondary Schools Council, 19 October 1968.

(1267) HIRST, J. A proposal for an integrated school library system for the public schools of New South Wales. Syd, School Library Assn of NSW, 1969. 31p. (School Library Association of New South Wales. Occasional Papers, no 6).

(1268) LIBRARY work with children: [papers from a seminar held on 19 April 1969]. Griffith, NSW, Riverina Regional Group, Library Assn of Aust, 1969. 21p.

(1269) NEW South Wales. Department of Education. Inservice Training Branch. The school library. Syd, [1969]. 13 leaves.

(1270) SCHOOL Library Association of New South Wales. Towards a national poli cy for school libraries. Syd, 1968. 14p. (School Library Association of New South Wales. Occasional Papers, no 7).

(1271) SCHOOL Library Association of Victoria. Annual Seminar, Swinburne College of Technology, 1969. Collection building; papers. Edited by J. Ward. Melb, 1969. 237 leaves.

(1272) SEMINAR on School Libraries, Sydney, 1968. [Papers]. Syd, Federation of Parents and Citizens Assns of NSW, 1969. 15p.

1970 (1273) AUSTRALIA. Department of Education and Science. The role of the principal and staff in an effective school library program. Canb, 1970. 7p.

(1274) BROWN, C.A. Libraries and education. Hawthorn, Vic, ACER, 1970. 69p. (Quarterly Review of Australian Education, vol 3 no 3).

(1275) SCHOOL Library Association of Victoria. Planning school libraries; report of a seminar at La Trobe University on 29 November 1969. Edited by J. Ward. Melb, 1970. 29p.

(1276) TRASK, M., editor. Planning of Australian school libraries; proceedings of the Seminar held at the University of NSW, Sydney, 7-8 July 1969. Syd, [Univ of NSW?], 1970. 72p.

(1277) VICTORIA. Education Department. Survey of primary school libraries 1970. Melb, 1970. 13p.

1971 (1278) AUSTRALIA. Secondary Schools Libraries Committee. Standards for secondary school libraries. [2nd edition]. Canb, Aust Govt Publishing Service, 1971. 54p.

(1279) NEW South Wales Teachers Federation. Secondary library survey, 1971. Syd, 1971. 13p.

(1280) THE ROLE of libraries in secondary education; Australian Unesco Seminar, University of NSW, August 1970. Canb, Aust Govt Publishing Service, 1971. 112p.

(1281) VICTORIA Institue of Colleges. Library Committee. Libraries in colleges of advanced education: a brief guide to their administration and function. Melb, 1971. 36p.

(1282) VICTORIAN Association of Students of Advanced Education. Library report. North Melb, 1971. 15 leaves.

1972 (1283) AUSTRALIAN School Library Association. School media centres, a response to change: [papers of the Second National Conference, Melbourne 1970]. Melb, 1972. 110p.

(1284) COHEN, D. Primary libraries: a report to the nation. Melb, Aust Library Promotion Council, 1972. 19p.

(1285) McNALLY, P.T. A guide to the practice of non book librarianship; a manual for the organisation and administration of non book materials and services in college of advanced education libraries. Toowoomba, Qld, Darling Downs Inst of Advanced Education, 1972. 133p.

(iv) Tests and Measurements

This section contains works on general aspects of testing and measuring, including examinations, assessments, moderation. For works that deal with tests in specific subjects, see the subject index under subject. For example, 'Evaluation of achievement in mathematics' is listed in the section that includes works on the teaching of mathematics.

1924 (1286) PHILLIPS, G. E. Measurement of general ability: an Australian revision and extension of the Binet-Simon scale. Syd, Teachers College Press, 1924. 2 vols.

1928 (1287) HANSEN, M. P. Public examinations and approval of secondary school courses in Victoria; a report. Melb, MUP, 1928. 71p.

1932 (1288) HALES, N. M. An advanced test of general intelligence. Melb, MUP, 1932. 63p. (ACER Educational Research Series, no 11).

1934 (1289) THREE studies in the comparative intelligence of English, American and Australian children. Melb, MUP, 1934. 70p. (ACER Educational Research Series, no 22).
Contents: A comparison of the intelligence of Victorian and American school children by R. D. Collmann; The standardization of Professor Spearman's 'Measure of intelligence' for metropolitan school children, Perth WA by A. J. Marshall; A standardization for Perth WA of the Sydney Teachers College Group Scale (Phillips Group Scale) by R. Thomas.

1935 (1290) COLLMANN, R. D. and Jorgensen, C. Three studies in the prediction of scholastic success. Melb, MUP, 1935. 68p. (ACER Educational Research Series, no 35).

(1291) MACINTYRE, G. A. and Wood, W. The standardization of an Australian reading test. Melb, MUP, 1935. 70p. (ACER Educational Research Series, no 39).

1936 (1292) SEITZ, J. A. Variability of examination results; a study of the public examinations by Victoria, 1922-33. Melb, MUP, 1936. 55p. (ACER Educational Research Series, no 43).

1938 (1293) CUNNINGHAM, K. S. Examinations in Australia. Lond, Evans, 1938. 27p.
Reprinted from the Year Book of Education, 1938.

(1294) CURTIN, J. P., editor. The problem of public examinations; containing a symposium by a group of Victorian educationists on suggested changes in the secondary examination system. Melb, Collegiate Press, 1938. 80p.

(1295) McINTYRE, G. A. The standardization of intelligence tests in Australia. Melb, MUP, 1938. 82p. (ACER Educational Research Series, no 54).
A supplement issued with this volume contains two sample tests and instructions for their use.

1940 (1296) KING, R. H. The nature and use of intelligence test results; a guide to teachers. Syd, R. Day, 1940. 7p.

1942 (1297) CUNNINGHAM, K. S. The scientific selection of personnel; an address delivered ... to the Institute of Industrial Management. Melb, Vic Chamber of Manufactures, 1942. 15p.

1944 (1298) AUSTRALIAN Council for Educational Research. Interim report on tests applied to first year students at Melbourne University, April 1943. Melb, 1944. 19 leaves.

1945 (1299) GASKING, D. A. T. Examinations and the aims of education. Carlton, Vic, MUP, 1945. 63p.
Second edition 1968.

1947 (1300) AUSTRALIAN Council for Educational Research. Accrediting for public examinations in Australia. Melb, 1947. 46p.

(1301) AUSTRALIAN Council for Educational Research. Errors in the marking of printed tests. Melb, 1947. 5 leaves. (Information Bulletin, no 9).

(1302) FREW, W. L. Pupils handbook to the Bursary examination. Syd, Whitcombe & Tombs, 1947. 128p.

1950 (1303) QUEENSLAND. Department of Public Instruction. Research and Guidance Branch. The prediction of secondary school examination success. Brisb, 1950. 45 leaves. (Bulletin no 1).

(1304) SCHONELL, F. J. and Schonell, F. E. Diagnostic and attainment testing, including a manual of tests, their nature, use, recording and interpretation. Edinb, Oliver and Boyd, 1950. 168p.
Third edition 1958.

1951 (1305) KEATS, J. A. A statistical theory of objective test scores. Melb, ACER, 1951. 48p.

(1306) QUEENSLAND. Department of Public Instruction. Research and Guidance Branch. Selection for secondary education in Queensland. Brisb, 1951. 33 leaves. (Bulletin no 4).

(1307) QUEENSLAND. Department of Public Instruction. Research and Guidance Branch. Summary of test research. Brisb, 1951. 27 leaves. (Bulletin no 5).

1953 (1308) KEATS, J. A. and Spearritt, D. Differences between two IQ estimates. Melb, ACER, 1953. 4 leaves. (Information Bulletin, no 27).

(1309) QUEENSLAND. Department of Public Instruction. Research and Guidance Branch. Investigations of clerical and shorthand aptitude. Brisb, 1953. 34 leaves. (Bulletin no 8).

(1310) SPEARRITT, D. and Keats, J. A. Longitudinal comparison of IQs given by intelligence tests at junior and intermediate levels. Melb, ACER, 1953. 12 leaves. (Information Bulletin, no 28).

1954 (1311) SPEARRITT, D. Preparation of test norms based on Victorian National Service Testing Programme, 1952-53. Melb, ACER, 1954. 26 leaves. (Information Bulletin, no 31).

1956 (1312) QUEENSLAND. Department of Public Instruction. Research and Guidance Branch. Summary of test research. Brisb, 1956. 25 leaves. (Bulletin no 12).

(1313) QUEENSLAND. Department of Public Instruction. Research and Guidance Branch. Tests and examinations in the prediction of academic success in the secondary school. Brisb, 1956. 36 leaves. (Bulletin no 11).

1958 (1314) AUSTRALIAN Council for Educational Research. Statistics of public and other examinations in Australia at secondary school level, 1950-57. Melb, 1958. 8 leaves.

(1315) SOUTH AUSTRALIA. Department of Education. Psychology Branch. Intelligence tests in primary schools. Adel, Govt Pr, 1958. 24p.

(1316) TECHNIQUES of examining at the secondary school level; a report. Brisb, Univ of Qld Faculty of Education, 1958. 55p. (Research Study, no 8).

1959 (1317) AUSTRALIAN Council for Educational Research. Some research in examining at matriculation level. Melb, [1959?]. 14 leaves.

(1318) QUEENSLAND. Department of Education. Research and Guidance Branch. A survey of teacher and student attitudes to the Junior Public Examination. Brisb, 1959. 81 leaves. (Bulletin no 18).

1962 (1319) AUSTRALIAN Council for Educational Research. Making the classroom test; a guide for teachers. Melb, 1962. 36p. 'Originally prepared by ... Educational Testing Service [USA], with suitable modification to meet local conditions' (preface).

(1320) DUNN, S. S. Testing in the primary school. Melb, ACER, 1962. 30p. (VIER Educational Pamphlet, no 3). 'A summary of a six-night lecture-discussion course organised by the Primary Education Today Group of the Victorian Institute of Educational Research' (foreword). 2nd edition 1972.

1964 (1321) AUSTRALIAN Council for Educational Research. Survey of general ability of pupils in forms 4, 5 and 6 of Victorian secondary schools in 1962. Hawthorn, Vic, 1964. 2 vols. Report no 1 by M. L. Turner. Report no 2 by W. C. Radford and T. S. Duff. (Issued as Memorandum Series, no 4).

(1322) EDGAR, D. E. Examination marks; their use and interpretation Melb, Hall's Book Store, 1964. 32p.

(1323) FRASER, I. C. Report to schools on the tryout of the trial forms of test L (Listening). Melb, ACER, 1964. 9 leaves.

(1324) THEOBALD, J. H. An introduction to the principles of classroom testing. Melb, Hall's Book Store, 1964. 82p.

1965 (1325) THE COMMONWEALTH Secondary Scholarships in Victoria, 1964; two-year scholarship awards. Hawthorn, Vic, ACER, 1965. 40p. (Memorandum Series, no 2).

(1326) HARRIES, W. T. The Illinois Test of Psycholinguistic Abilities (ITPA); an appraisal. Hawthorn, Vic, ACER, 1965. 19p. (Memorandum no 1).

(1327) WESTERN Australia. Department of Education. Statement on the mental abilities and learning of the school child; an appraisal of research evidence, with implications for the primary school curriculum, compiled by L. Pond. Perth, Govt Pr, 1965. 36p.

1966 (1328) AUSTRALIAN Council for Educational Research. Statement of educational objectives being tested in the Commonwealth Secondary Scholarship examination, prepared by T. M. Whitford and others. Melb, 1966. 16 leaves.

(1329) QUEENSLAND. Board of Junior Secondary School Studies. Examining in the secondary school; a guide to the purposes and construction of examinations. Brisb, 1966. 20p.

1967 (1330) ANDERSON, D. S. and Western, J. S. An inventory to measure students attitudes. St Lucia, Qld, Univ of Qld Press, 1967. 23p. (Queensland University Department of History. Papers, vol 1 no 3).

(1331) DUNN, S. S. Measurement and evaluation in the secondary school. Hawthorn, Vic, ACER, 1967. 141p. (Monographs on Secondary Education, no 3).
Second edition 1970.

(1332) RENEHAN, W. T., Arney, D. J. and McBean, N. E. Report on 1965 Victorian primary schools testing programme. Hawthorn, Vic, ACER, 1967. 31p. (Memorandum Series, no 7).

(1333) RENEHAN, W. T. and Watson, E. Report on 1966. Victorian primary schools testing programme. Hawthorn, Vic, ACER, 1967. 23p. (Memorandum Series, no 8).

1968 (1334) MADDERN, I. T. The trouble with examinations. [Morwell, Vic, the Author, 1968?]. 20p.

(1335) RECHTER, B. and Wilson, N. L. Examining for university entrance in Australia; current practices. Hawthorn, Vic, ACER, 1968. 27p. (Quarterly Review of Australian Education, vol 2, no 2).

(1336) RENEHAN, W. T. and Watson, E. Report on 1967 Victorian primary schools testing programme. Hawthorn, Vic, ACER, 1968. 31p. (Memorandum Series, no 9).

1969 (1337) AUSTRALIAN College of Education. Conference, 10th, Adelaide, 1969. Educational measurement and assessment, Carlton, Vic, 1969. 163p.

(1338) EDWARDS, J. A. Multiple choice tests; an automated examination procedure. Bundoora, Vic, La Trobe Univ Computer Centre, 1969. 7p. (Application Note, no 1).

1969 (1339) QUEENSLAND. Department of Education. Research and Curriculum Branch. Standards of achievement in reading, spelling and certain study skills, Queensland Grade 7 pupils. Brisb, 1969. 31p. (Bulletin, no 36).

(1340) SEMINAR on examining and other forms of assessment in the Australian National University, Canberra, 1969. Papers, Canb, 1969. 66p.

(1341) VICTORIAN Universities and Schools Examinations Board. Report on the pilot scheme in moderating, 1968, edited by R. G. Rowlands. Melb, 1969. 27p.

(1342) VICTORIAN Universities and Schools Examinations Board. A second report on the pilot scheme in moderating; some practical problems, [edited by R. G. Rowlands]. Melb, 1969. 16 leaves.

(1343) WILSON, N. A study of test-retest and of marker reliabilities of the 1966 Commonwealth Secondary Scholarship Examination (CSSE). Hawthorn, Vic, ACER, 1969. 18p. (Information Bulletin, no 50).

1970 (1344) DE LEMOS, M. M. A study of the factors affecting performance on the Piaget Conservation tests; the effects of questioning. Hawthorn, Vic, ACER, 1970. (Progress Report, no 1).

(1345) QUEENSLAND. Department of Education. Research and Curriculum Branch. Research findings relating to some aspects of the Commonwealth Secondary Scholarship Scheme in Queensland. Brisb, 1970. 75p. (Bulletin no 37).

(1346) RECHTER, B. Admission to tertiary studies; an account of an experimental test battery and a proposal for its use. Hawthorn, Vic, ACER, 1970. 60p. (Occasional Paper, no 2).

(1347) WILSON, N. Objective tests and mathematical learning. Hawthorn, Vic, ACER, 1970. 130p.

1971 (1348) KEATS, J. A. An introduction to quantitative psychology. Syd, Wiley, 1971. 138p.

(1349) MOORE, W. E. Evaluation and selection practices in Australia and overseas; paper presented at the National Conference of Examining Bodies, Sydney 1971. Syd, Education Dept Centre for Research in Measurement and Evaluation, 1971. 20 leaves.

(1350) MOORE, W. E. Why alternatives to public examinations; paper presented at the National Conference of Examining Bodies, Sydney 1971. Syd, Education Dept Centre for Research in Measurement and Evaluation, 1971. 13 leaves.

(1351) QUEENSLAND. Department of Education. Research and Curriculum Branch. The performance of Queensland Grade 12 students on the Australian Scholastic Aptitude Test. Brisb, 1971. 35p. (Queensland Grade 12 Study Report, no 1).

(1352) QUEENSLAND. Department of Education. Research and Curriculum Branch. School assessment procedures, 2. The multiple choice item. Brisb, 1971. 62p.

(1353) SOUTH Australia. Education Department. Research and Planning Branch. Alternatives to the matriculation examination in South Australia. Adel, 1971. 15p.

(1354) SUTHERLAND, J. E. N. Tertiary Education Entrance Project: interim report on the evaluation of the TEEP Series A test battery. Canb, Dept of Education and Science, 1971. 68 leaves.

(1355) VICTORIA. Education Department. An appraisal of the Illinois Test of Psycholinguistic Abilities, by D. M. Pickering. Melb, 1971. 38p. (RR 2/71).

(1356) WILKES, R. E. , Noble, T. E. and Renehan, W. T. Some effects of winning a Commonwealth Secondary Scholarship award; a follow-up study. Hawthorn, Vic, ACER, 1971. 45p. (Research Series, no 87).

1972 (1357) QUEENSLAND. Department of Education. Research and Curriculum Branch. Moderation within schools. Brisb, 1972. 65p. (Schools Assessment Procedures, no 4).

(1358) QUEENSLAND. Department of Education. Research and Curriculum Branch. Proposals for the compilation of an order of merit for grade 12 students. Brisb, 1972. 4p.

(1359) RENEHAN, W. T. The predictive validity of the 1964 Commonwealth Secondary Scholarship Examination; the report of a follow-up study of candidates for one-year scholarships at the 1964 Commonwealth Secondary Scholarship Examination in Victoria. Hawthorn, Vic, ACER, 1972. 15p. (Research Series, no 88).

(1360) SCHOOLS Board of Tasmania. The School Certificate. Hobart, 1972. 16p.

(1361) WILKES, R. E. and Noble, T. E. The predictive validity of the 1966 Commonwealth Secondary Scholarship awards; the report of a follow up study of candidates for Commonwealth Secondary Scholarship awards in South Australia, New South Wales and Victoria. Hawthorn, Vic, ACER, 1972. 42p. (Research series, no 90).

(1362) WILSON, N. Assessment in the primary school. Adel, Education Dept Research & Planning Branch, 1972. 49p.

5 Students

This chapter contains sections on (i) students at school; (ii) school leavers; (iii) students at colleges and universities; (iv) overseas students in Australia; (v) graduates.

(i) Students at School

Includes works on behaviour and discipline.

1934 (1363) CLARKE, G. Some character traits of delinquent and normal children in terms of perseveration factor. Melb, MUP, 1934. 42p. (ACER Educational Research Series, no 29).

1935 (1364) GUTTERIDGE, M. V. The duration of attention in young children. Melb, MUP, 1935. 52p. (ACER Educational Research Series, no 41).

1936 (1365) HILL, M. Training to reason; an investigation into the possibility of training in seeing relations in evidence. Melb, MUP, 1936. 71p. (ACER Educational Research Series, no 44).

1937 (1366) WOODS, M. T. Juvenile delinquency, with special reference to institutional treatment. Melb, MUP, 1937. 80p. (ACER Educational Research Series, no 50).

1942 (1367) MUHL, A. M. Truants: culprits or victims? Melb, Left Book Club of Victoria, 1942. 49p.

1946 (1368) SCHNIERER, I. Children's entertainment. Melb, ACER, 1946. 52p. (Future of Education Series, no 11).
'... entertainment is part of education, and education and entertainment can be interlocked to their mutual advantage'.

1949 (1369) AN EXAMINATION of some aspects of grade placement of children. Melb, ACER, [1949]. 18 leaves. (Information Bulletin, no 17).

1954 (1370) RADFORD, W. C. Some sex differences in the infant school. Melb, ACER, 1954. 4 leaves. (Information Bulletin, no 32).

1957 (1371) CONNELL, W. F., Francis, E. P. and Skilbeck, E. E. Growing up in an Australian city; a study of adolescents in Sydney. Melb, ACER, 1957. 255p. (Educational Research Series, no 72).

1960 (1372) RADFORD, W. C. School pupils and school leavers in five states; estimations of numbers from successive 13-year old generations of school children who will continue at and leave school. Melb, ACER, 1960. 19 leaves. (Information Bulletin, no 42).

1962 (1373) AUSTRALIAN Council for Educational Research. Seminar on Individual Differences, Melbourne 1962. The psychological facts of individual differences; statement prepared by Queensland group. Melb, 1962. 62 leaves.

(1374) CAMPBELL, W. J. and Keogh, R. Television and the Australian adolescent. Syd, A & R, 1962. 151p.

1963 (1375) TIERNEY, L. Children who need help; a study of child welfare policy and administration in Victoria. Melb, MUP, 1963. 128p.

1964 (1376) AUSTRALIAN Council for Educational Research. Survey of general ability of pupils in forms 4, 5 and 6 of Victorian secondary schools 1962; report no 1. A report prepared by the ... Council ... for the Victorian Minister of Education's Standing Committee on Senior Secondary and Tertiary Education. Melb , [1964]. 14p.

1965 (1377) BALSON, M. The effect of social-class membership on certain aspects of school performance and educational expectations of students and parents in the Geelong area. Clayton, Vic, Faculty of Education Monash Univ, 1965. 15p. (Research Bulletin, no 1).

1966 (1378) RADFORD, W. C. Staying longer at school; an examination of some statistics of enrolments and discussion of certain features of the tendency to stay longer at school. Hawthorn, Vic, ACER, 1966. 44p. (Information Bulletin, no 47).

1968 (1379) AUSTRALIA. Department of Education and Science. Territorial Education Branch. Survey of usual method of travel to school 1968. Canb, 1969. 6 leaves.

1969 (1380) BARROW, L. N. Preparing your child for school. Syd, Reed, 1969. 67p.

(1381) MEARES, A. D. Student problems and a guide to study. Melb, Hawthorn Press, 1969. 108p.

1970 (1382) COLEMAN, P. School power in Australia. Syd, the Author, 1970. 40p.

(1383) VICTORIA. Education Department. An account of parent involvement practices at Maryvale High School. Melb, 1970. 53p.

1971 (1384) BOURKE, S. F. and Naylor, D. R. The effects of school changes on army dependent children. Canb, 1971. 132 leaves and appendices. (Army School of Education Research Cell Project 4/70).

(1385) CHRISTIE, D. B. Survey by the Ryde Rotary Club on the number of 'latchkey children' attending schools in the Ryde municipality, 1971. Syd, Dept of Public Health, 1971 . 10 leaves.

(1386) EBBECK, F. N. and Gibson, G. W., editors. Education and the child. Syd, A & R, 1971. 160p.

(1387) GAUDRY, E. and Spielberger, C. D. Anxiety and educational achievement. Syd, Wiley, 1971. 182p.
Part 2: selected readings.

(1388) GENN, J. M. School-to-university transition as a change of environmental press. St Lucia, Qld, Univ of Qld Press, 1971. (Univ of Qld Papers. Faculty of Education vol 2, no 1).

(1389) HAMMOND, S. B. and Gleser, H. Mass media preference in adolescence; a study in changing tastes. Melb, Australian Broadcasting Control Board, 1971. 15p.

(1390) NIXON, M. Children's classification skills. Hawthorn, Vic, ACER, 1971. 107p. (Research Series, no 86).

(1391) ORD, I. G. Psychological test programmes and school certificate and university preliminary year results; some findings in Papua and New Guinea. Port Moresby, Psychological Services Branch, Dept of the Public Service Board, Papua New Guinea, 1971. 41p. (Research Report, no 2).

(1392) PAPUA New Guinea. Manpower Planning Unit. Office of Programming and Co-ordination. Longitudinal study of the 1969 School Certificate Examiners; report no 2). Port Moresby, 1971. 48 leaves. (Manpower Studies, no 4).

(1393) POWELL, R. J. Television viewing by young secondary students; a study of the television viewing behaviour of children at form two level. Melb, Aust Broadcasting Control Board, 1971. 34 leaves.

(1394) SOUTH Australia. Education Department. Research and Planning Branch. Report of a study in progress; the pilot stage of 'How children talk in school' (Preparatory grade). Adel, 1971. 14 leaves.

(1395) VICTORIA. Education Department. An evaluation and comparison of the behavioural profiles of special school children and primary school children classified as either readers or retarded readers, by S. Sykes. Melb, 1971. 42p. (RR 3/71).

(1396) VICTORIA. Education Department. An exmaination of the psycholinguistic abilities and disabilities of Grade 2 children of differing socio-economic status and ethnic background, Greek and Australian, by D. M. Pickering. Melb, 1971. 27p. (RR 10/71).

(1397) VICTORIA. Education Department. Primary school television survey 1970, compiled by I. B. Hargrave, Education Department Liaison Officer with the Australian Broadcasting Commission. [Melb, 1971]. 15p.

(1398) WESTERN Australia. Education Department. Outdoor education. Perth, 1971. 29 p.

1972 (1399) ANDERSON, D.S. and Beswick, D.G. Canberra secondary
school student survey 1972; the proposal to introduce fifth and
sixth form colleges in the ACT. First Report. Canberra, Education
Research Unit, Research School of the Social Sciences, ANU, 1972.
43p.

(1400) KEEVES, J.P. Educational environment and student
achievement; a multivariate study of the contributions of the home,
the school and the peer group to change in mathematics and science
performance during the first year at secondary school. Stockholm,
Almquist and Wiksell, 1972. 310p. (ACER Research Series, no 89).

(1401) NAYLOR, F.D. Personality and educational achievement.
Syd, Wiley, 1972. 162p.

(1402) ROWELL, J.A. and Selge, H. An investigation of the
effects of different rates and methods of promotion from infant
grades on the subsequent performances of children in South
Australian schools. Adel, Research and Planning Branch,
Education Dept of SA, 1972. 29p.

(1403) THOMSON, R.J. Television crime drama; a report to
the Australian Broadcasting Control Board on results and findings
of an experimental investigation ... into the effects on adolescents
and children of television crime dramas and tension films. [Melb],
Aust Broadcasting Control Board, 1972. 272p.

(1404) VICTORIA. Education Department. Curriculum and
Research Branch. Factors affecting student learning, by K. Blanchford
Melb, 1972. 16p. (Occasional Paper, no 4).

(1405) VICTORIA. Education Department. Curriculum and Research
Branch. Values and education, by K. Blachford. Melb, 1972. 18p.
(Occasional Paper, no 1).

(ii) School Leavers

Includes works on articulation and vocational guidance.

1932 (1406) GILES, G.R. and Lyall, J.R. Occupations in Victoria; an
investigation into the normal annual absorptive capacity of occupations in Victoria. Melb, MUP, 1932. 77p. (ACER Educational
Research Series, no 10).

1939 (1407) FENNER, C. Some aspects of the transition from school
to workshop. Melb, MUP for ACER, 1939. 19p.
Paper read before the Education Section of ANZAAS, Canberra,
January 1939.

1944 (1408) O'NEIL, W.M. From school to work; a plea for vocational
guidance. Melb, ACER, 1944. 40p. (Future of Education Series,
no 6).

1945 (1409) AUSTRALIAN Council for Educational Research. Vocational guidance in Australia. Melb, 1945. 4 leaves.

(1410) MOREY, E. A. The school leaving age. Melb, ACER, 1945. 42p. (Future of Education Series, no 9).

1947 (1411) HALL, H. L. Avenues for boys. Melb, the Author, 1947. 31p.

1950 (1412) QUEENSLAND. Department of Public Instruction. Research and Guidance Branch. The occupations entered by secondary school leavers, 1949. Brisb, 1950. 17 leaves. (Bulletin no 2).

1951 (1413) CATHOLIC Vocational Guidance Auxiliary. Vocational guidance for Catholic boys and girls; compiled by L. J. Muir. 2nd edition. Melb, Catholic Education Office, 1951. 64p.

1956 (1414) BERDIE, R. F. Manpower and the schools. Melb, ACER, 1956. 108p.

(1415) CONFERENCE on careers between Victorian secondary schools and the University of Melbourne, October 1956. Report. Melb, Univ Appointments Board, 1956. 41p.

1957 (1416) AUSTRALIAN Council for Educational Research. The education of the adolescent; documents prepared for the consideration of the Council at the annual meeting 29-30 August 1957. Melb, 1957. 1 vol.

1958 (1417) ODDIE, N. M. and Spearritt, D. Some activities of Australian adolescents. Melb, ACER, 1958-59. 3 vols. Contents: vol 1. The educational activities of Victorian adolescents; vol 2. The occupational activities of Australian adolescents; vol 3. Some occupational characteristics of Victorian male adolescents.

(1418) RADFORD, W. C. Some characteristics of students proceeding to higher technical education. Melb, ACER, 1958. 5 leaves. (Information Bulletin, no 36).

1959 (1419) MITCHELL, A. W. and Belshaw, R. R. The key to your career. Melb, Hall's Book Store, 1959. 479p.

1960 (1420) AUSTRALIAN Council for Educational Research. [Survey of pupils leaving school] from 1 April 1959 to 31 March 1960; ages, months of leaving, and destinations of students leaving government schools, New South Wales; interim report no 1. Melb, 1961. 6 leaves.

(1421) PROBLEMS of transition from secondary school to university: a conference of secondary schools and the university held at the University of Melbourne on 4 September 1959; convened by the University of Melbourne Appointments Board. Melb, MUP, 1960. 63p.

(1422) QUEENSLAND. Department of Education. Research and Guidance Branch. The college achievement and occupations entered by Queensland Agricultural High School and College leavers, 1955-59. Brisb, 1960. 13 leaves. (Bulletin no 20).

1961 (1423) AUSTRALIAN Council for Educational Research. Survey of pupils leaving school from 1 April 1959 - 31 March 1960 inclusive, from government schools in New South Wales, Victoria, Queensland, Western Australia, Tasmania; interim report no 2. Melb, 1961. 23 leaves.

(1424) AUSTRALIAN Council for Educational Research. Survey of pupils leaving school from government schools in South Australia; secondary schools, 1 April 1959 to 31 March 1960, primary schools 1 October 1958 to 30 September 1959; interim report no 3 Melb, 1961. 13 leaves.

(1425) AUSTRALIAN Council for Educational Research. Survey of pupils leaving school between 1 April 1959 and 31 March 1960 from non-government schools in all states; interim report no 4. Melb, 1961. 40 leaves.

(1426) MATRICULATION - and after; a survey of pupils in Australia who, in the 1957 examinations, qualified to matriculate to Australian universities, by the Commonwealth Office of Education and Australian Council for Educational Research. Melb, ACER, 1961. 102p.

1962 (1427) BUCKMAN, N. Some aspects of early leaving; a review of research. Melb, ACER, 1962. 81p.

(1428) QUEENSLAND. Department of Education. Research and Guidance Branch. The wastage of academically talented pupils in Queensland schools. Brisb, 1962. 70 leaves. (Bulletin no 24).

(1429) RADFORD, W. C. School leavers in Australia, 1959-60. Melb, ACER, 1962. 144p. (Educational Research Series, no 75).

1963 (1430) PROBLEMS of transition from school to university; report of a workshop held at the University of Western Australia, 5-6 August 1963. Perth, Univ of WA, 1963. 65p.

1964 (1431) NEW South Wales. Vocational Guidance Bureau. [Work of the] Vocational Guidance Bureau, Syd, 1964. 7p.
Vocational guidance leaflets are also issued.

1966 (1432) DAVIS, L., compiler. Careers in Australia; a list of selected references. Melb, State Library of Vic, 1966. 63p. (Research Service Bibliographies 1966, no 6).

1967 (1433) AUSTRALIA. Department of the Interior. Education Branch. School leaver survey, 1967. Canb, 1967. 19p.

(1434) WALKER, W. G., editor. School to university. Armidale, NSW, Dept of Education, Univ of New England, 1967. 95p. (New England Papers on Education, no 2).
A report of the proceedings of the High School Principals Conference held at the University of New England from 31 May to 2 June 1967.

1969 (1435) DUNN, S. S. and others. A study of the choice of tertiary education by 5th and 6th form males in Victoria. Clayton, Vic, Faculty of Education Monash Univ, 1969. 191p.
Sponsored by the Commonwealth Advisory Committee on Advanced Education.

1971 (1436) ANDERSON, A. W. and Collins, N. R. A survey of school estimates of student performance: interim report on estimates of performance in the 1970 leaving and matriculation examinations and qualifying for university entry. Nedlands, WA, Research Unit in Univ Education, Univ of WA, 1971. 12 leaves.

(1437) UNESCO Youth Research Project in Australia. A basis for youth work in Australia. Canb, Aust Govt Publishing Service, 1971. 43p.

(iii) Students at Colleges and Universities

1945 (1438) MITCHELL, F. W. Student health; [an address]. Adel, Univ of Adel, 1945. 15p.

1947 (1439) WALSHE, R. D. Student work for progress. Syd, Acacia Press, 1947. 46p.

(1440) HOHNE, H. H. The prediction of academic success; an investigation into the academic careers of students entering the University of Melbourne in 1943 and 1944. Melb, ACER, 1950-51. 2 vols.

(1441) CUNNINGHAM, K. S. Success and failure in Australian universities. Melb, ACER, 1953. 12 leaves.

1955 (1442) HOHNE, H. H. Success and failure in scientific faculties of the University of Melbourne. Melb, ACER, 1955. 136p.

1958 (1443) FELS, R. M. Report of the Asian study seminar, Aloka, Ceylon, July 28 - September 6 1958. Maitland, NSW, NUAUS, 1958. 20p.
Seminar conducted by the Co-ordinating Secretariat of the International Student Conference and by the Ceylon University Students Federation.

(1444) SANDERS, C. Report on academic wastage and failure among university students in Australia and other countries, 1928-58; a review of research and opinion. Perth, Faculty of Education Univ of WA, 1958. 47p.

1959 (1445) NATIONAL Union of Australian University Students. The fifth and sixth International Students Conference in Japan; an account by the Australian delegates. Syd, 1959. 28p.

(1446) NATIONAL Union of Australian University Students. Students in India, 1959; report of a delegation from NUAUS. Newcastle, NSW, 1959. 54p.

1960 (1447) HUGHES, P. W. Academic achievement at the university; an analysis of factors related to success. Hobart, Univ of Tas, 1960. 103p.

(1448) HUGHES, P. W. Statistics of academic progress, 1950-59. Hobart, Univ of Tas, 1960. 56p.

1961 (1449) THEOBOLD, M. J. A study of some first year students at the University of Melbourne. Melb, NUAUS, 1961. 120p.

(1450) THEOBOLD, M. J. and Evans, G. Taxation and the student; a statement of the policy of the National Union of Australian University Students on those aspects of the taxation legislation of the Commonwealth of Australia which pertain to tertiary students. Melb, NUAUS, 1961. 21p.

1964 (1451) GRAY, G. A. and Underwood, K. L. Survey of student needs, Newcastle University College. Syd, Univ of NSW, 1964. 104p. (New South Wales University Student Counselling and Research Unit, Bulletin no 1).

(1452) MELBOURNE. University. Students Representative Council. Melbourne University: a student report; memorandum to the Council of the University of Melbourne. Melb, 1964. 21p.

1965 (1453) KATZ, C. N. , Katz, F. M. and Olphert, W. B. What happens to students; a study of students at the University of New England, 1961-64. Armidale, NSW, UNE Student Research Unit, 1965. 150p.

1966 (1454) APPLEYARD, R. T. A survey of Ph D candidates and first class honours graduates in the humanities and social sciences in Australian state universities, July 1966. Canb, Research School of the Social Sciences ANU, 1966. 24p.
Includes 13 pages of tables.

(1455) BARNARD, P. D. and Siu, S. K. Academic performance of dental students. Syd, Univ of Syd Dept of Preventive Dentistry, 1966. 30p.

(1456) TASMANIA. University. Union. Students Representative Council. University education; a survey of student opinion. Hobart, 1966. 76p.

1967 (1457) DUNSTAN, M. Scholastic types among college students. Kensington, NSW, Educational Research Unit, Univ of NSW, 1967. 22p. (Occasional Publication, no 3).

(1458) ROGERS, B. A preliminary geographical investigation of student origins and university catchment areas in New South Wales. Armidale, NSW, Dept of Geography Univ of New England, 1967. 105p.

1968 (1459) MITCHELL, A. G. and Cohen, S. W. The Australian university student; admission, selection and progress. Canb, Aust Vice-Chancellors Committee, 1968. 37p.

1969 (1460) AUSTRALIAN National University, Canberra. Students Representative Council. Submission to University Council on student participation in university government. Canb, 1969. 7p.

(1461) NATIONAL Union of Australian University Students. Education and taxation; a submission·concerning increased taxation benefits for students. North Melb, 1969. 9 leaves.

(1462) JONES, E. H. A report of an investigation into first admissions into tertiary educational institutions in 1970. Perth, Tertiary Education Commission of WA, 1970. 20 leaves.

1970 (1463) MADDOX, H. Students entering applied science in colleges of advanced education; a study of their social origins, educational background and motivation. Canb, ANU, 1970. 286p. (Research School of Social Sciences Education Research Unit, Occasional Report no 1).

(1464) NATIONAL Union of Australian University Students. Education Department. Education policy. Melb, 1970. 27p.

(1465) NEW England, NSW. University. Educational Research Unit. First-year intake, 1970. Armidale, NSW, 1970 . 6p.

1971 (1466) ANDERSON, A. W. Aggregate scores and university selection. Nedlands, WA, Research Unit in Univ Education, Univ of WA, 1971. 12 leaves.

(1467) AUSTRALIA. Department of Education and Science. The 1961 study; an analysis of the progress of new bachelor degree entrants to Australian universities in 1961. Prepared for the Australian Vice-Chancellors Committee. Canb, 1971. 297p.

(1468) AUSTRALIAN Union of Students. Commonwealth scholarships submission, 1971. North Melb, 1971. 39 leaves.

(1469) AUSTRALIAN Union of Students. Education and fighting policies, 1971. North Melb, 1971. 34 p.

(1470) BARRETT, E. M. Part time students at the University of New South Wales. Syd, Univ of NSW Tertiary Education Research Centre, 1971. 15p. (Monograph no 2).

(1471) GAUSSEN, R. and Tomasello, R. Taxation and the tertiary student; a submission to point out anomalies existing in the taxation structure relating to tertiary students and their parents. Melb, AUS, 1971. 15p.

(1472) NATIONAL Conference of Colleges of Advanced Education Students, Melbourne 1971. Proceedings. [Melb, 1971?]. 1 vol (various pagination).

(1473) PAPUA New Guinea. Manpower Planning Unit. Office of Programming and Co-ordination. Analysis of inputs to tertiary institutions. 1971. 27 leaves. (Manpower Studies, no 3).

(1474) UNDERWOOD, K. L. Full-time undergraduate costs and income, 1970. Kensington, NSW, Univ of NSW Student Counselling and Research Unit, 1971. 53p. (Bulletin no 4).

(1475) UNDERWOOD, K. L. Internal validity of measures of vocational interest. Kensington, NSW, Univ of NSW Student Counselling and Research Unit, 1971. 63p. (Bulletin no 3, 1971).

(1476) WESTERN Australian Tertiary Education Commission. Seminar on admission to tertiary institutions in Western Australia: present problems and future implications, 19 and 20 March 1971. Perth, 1971. 3 papers bound together.

(1477) WOOD, W. Comparative study of scholastic attainments and abilities of students entering tertiary education in Queensland. [Brisb, Board of Advanced Education, 1971]. 22p. Address delivered at the 43rd ANZAAS Congress, Brisbane, May 1971.

1972 (1478) AUSTRALIA. Department of Education and Science. Report on pros and cons of student loans, by W. J. Weeden. Canb, 1972. 65p.

(1479) KATZ, F. M. and Barrett, E. M. Two and a half years later. Kensington, NSW, Tertiary Education Research Centre, Univ of NSW, 1972. 23p. (Monograph no 4).

(1480) PAPUA New Guinea. Manpower Planning Unit. Office of Programming and Co-ordination. Analysis of inputs to tertiary institutions, 1972. Port Moresby, 1972. 32 leaves. (Manpower Studies, no 5).

(1481) WESTERN Australian Tertiary Education Commission. Report by Research Officer on new enrolments in Western Australian tertiary institutions, 1972. Perth, 1972. 30p.

(iv) Overseas Students in Australia

1953 (1482) AUSTRALIAN Council for Educational Research. SE Asian students. Melb, 1953. 7 leaves. Report of a survey on the performance of South East Asian students at the University of Melbourne.

1966 (1483) ADAM, R. The academic background of Asian students in Australian universities. [the Author? 1966?]. 21p. Sponsored by Social Science Research Council of Australia, NUAUS and University of Western Australia.

(1484) HODGKIN, M. C. Australian training and Asian living.
Perth, Univ of WA Press, 1966. 233p.

1967 (1485) CANBERRA Council for Overseas Students. International
Centre Sub-Committee. Report on the need for an overseas students
centre in Canberra. Canb, 1967. 16p.

(1486) CONFERENCE of Co-ordinating Committees and Welfare
Officers, Canberra, 1967. Welfare of overseas students. Canb,
Dept of External Affairs, 1967. 1 vol (various pagination).

1968 (1487) AUSTRALIA. Department of Immigration. Private overseas
students in Australia. Canb, Govt Pr, 1968. 20p.

(1488) OVERSEAS Students Service. A basis of understanding;
edited by P. Boddy and Dur-e Dara. Melb, 1968. 12p.

1969 (1489) KEATS, D. H. Back in Asia; a follow up study of Australian
trained Asian students. Canb, Dept of Economics Research School
of Pacific Studies ANU, 1969. 199p.

1972 (1490) HODGKIN, M. C. The innovators; the role of foreign
trained persons in Southeast Asia. Syd Univ Press, 1972. 127p.

(v) Graduates

1953 (1491) CONFERENCE between University of Melbourne Appointments
Board and Employers, Melbourne, November 1952 - March 1953.
Training schemes for graduates; a report. Melb, the Board, 1953.
38p.

1954 (1492) BUTTEN, E. E. Training of graduates in commerce and
industry. Melb, Appointments Board, Univ of Melb, 1954. 16p.

1959 (1493) RORKE, M. W. The vocational contributions of women
graduates of the University of Queensland. Brisb, Qld Univ Press,
1959. 20p. (University of Queensland Papers, Faculty of Education
vol 1, no 1).

1965 (1494) DAWSON, M., compiler. Graduate and married; a report
on a survey of one thousand and seventy married women graduates
of the University of Sydney, edited by J. Rorke. Syd, Univ of
Syd Dept of Adult Education, 1965. 223p.

1966 (1495) PUNCH, K. F. Some factors associated with the output of
graduates from Australian universities; a survey and analysis of
recent research. Perth, Univ of WA, 1966. 92p.

1967 (1496) AUSTRALIAN Federation of University Graduates. Graduate
organisations in Australia. Syd, 1967. 26p.

1968 (1497) GOUGH, J. E. and Rawling, S. J. Graduation and employment;
a study of the destinations of graduates of the Australian National
University 1968. Canb, Univ Counselling Service ANU, 1968. 77p.
(Counselling and Appointments Studies, no 1).

(1498) GRAVELL, K. Survey of commerce graduates, 1950-65.
Melb, MUP, 1968. 36p.

(1499) MENZIES, Sir R. G. [The post-graduate student. Syd],
Inst of Radio and Electronics Engineers, Australia, 1968. 15p.
(Dunrossil Memorial Lecture, 2nd, 1968).

1969 (1500) MACQUARIE University, Sydney. The Macquarie University
graduate and the employer. North Ryde, NSW, 1969. 44p.

1970 (1501) ANDERSON, D. S. and Western, J. S. Social profiles of
students in four professions. Hawthorn, Vic, ACER, 1970. 38p.
(Quarterly Review of Australian Education, vol 3, no 4).
Contains Supplement (pages 29-38) on 'Social origins of college
engineering students' by B. C. Horne.

(1502) DUNN, S. S., Fensham, P. J. and Strong, P. J. Engineers
look back; a study of the views of recent diplomates and graduates
on their tertiary education and its employment implications.
[Clayton, Vic, Monash Univ, 1970]. 104p.

(1503) McGRATH, A. G. A short history of the NSW Association
of University Women Graduates; Part 1 (1882-1920). Syd,
NSW Assn of Univ Women Graduates, 1970. 33p.

(1504) PATON, I. G. F. After graduation: a survey of the occupations of graduates of Flinders University of South Australia,
1970. [Bedford Park, SA, Flinders Univ, 1971?]. 24p.

(1505) RAWLING, S. J. Destinations of graduates of Australian
National University, 1969. Canb, ANU, 1970. 16p.

1971 (1506) ILBERY, J., Nelson, H. and Simons, D. Qualification:
BA; an independent survey of the 1969 arts graduates of Sydney
University. Syd, Univ of Syd, [1971?]. 42p.

(1507) WESTERN Australia. University Counselling Service.
Graduate employment 1971; a survey of the occupations of graduates
of the University of Western Australia, whose degrees or diplomas
were conferred in 1971. Nedlands, WA, 1971. 24p.

1972 (1508) WARK, I. W. The employment of graduates and their
functions in the community. [Univ of Syd, 1972]. 10 leaves.

(1509) WESTERN Australia. University Counselling Service.
Graduate employment 1972; a survey of the occupations of
graduates of the University of WA, whose degrees or diplomas
were conferred in 1972. [Nedlands, WA], 1972. 24p.

6 Schools

This chapter contains sections on (i) Australian schools; (ii) private schools; (iii) histories of state schools; (iv) histories of private schools.

(i) Australian Schools

Includes works on administration of schools and school buildings.

1936 (1510) CRAMER, J. F. Australian schools through American eyes. Melb, MUP, 1936. 59p. (ACER Educational Research Series, no 42).

1945 (1511) STATE School Teachers Union of WA. Western Australia's high schools must be improved. Perth, 1945. 10p.

1948 (1512) OPINIONS of Victorian teachers on co-education. Melb, ACER, 1948. 7 leaves. (Information Bulletin, no 11).

(1513) PRIESTLEY, R. and Woodberry, L. School buildings and equipment. Melb, MUP for ACER, 1948. 86p.

(1514) VICTORIA. Education Department. Consolidated schools in Victoria. Melb, Education Dept, 1948. 4 leaves.

(1515) WHITFORD, R. L. The community school. Hobart, Govt Pr, 1948. 7p.

1958 (1516) KEATS, J. A. and Duff, T. S. Characteristics of a desirable classroom. Melb, ACER, 1958. 18 leaves. (Information Bulletin, no 35).

1959 (1517) AUSTRALIAN Council for Educational Research. Australian school enrolments; a compilation of enrolment data showing the numbers enrolled in government and non-government schools in Australia at successive ages on or about August 1956, and in earlier years. Melb, 1959. 84p.

1960 (1518) RUSSELL, H. L. A guide to the preparation of a secondary school time-table. Melb, Vic Secondary Teachers Assn, 1960. 9p.

1961 (1519) CONFERENCE on School Administration, University of Queensland, 1961. Papers and proceedings, edited by G. W. Bassett. Brisb, Univ of Qld, Dept of Education, 1961. 197p.

1962 (1520) WYNDHAM, H. S. The search for better schools. [Syd, the Author, 1962?]. 13p.

1963 (1521) BASSETT, G. W. , Crane, A. R. and Walker, W. G.
Headmasters for better schools. Brisb, Univ of Qld Press, 1963.
114p.
Second edition 1967.

(1522) RUSSELL, H. L. and others. Planning time tables. Melb,
Vic Secondary Teachers Assn, 1963. 35p.

1965 (1523) WALKER, W. G. , editor. The principal at work; case
studies in school administration. Brisb, Univ of Qld Press, 1965.
228p.
Second edition 1968.

1966 (1524) AUSTIN, A. G. The Australian school. Croydon, Vic,
Longmans, 1966. 64p. (Australian Landmarks Series).
A brief history for secondary school children.

(1525) QUEENSLAND. Department of Education. Research and
Curriculum Branch. An evaluation of a non-graded organisation
in a large Queensland primary school. Brisb, 1966. 31 leaves.
(Bulletin no 31).

1967 (1526) CUNNINGHAM, K. S. and Ross, D. J. An Australian school
at work. Hawthorn, Vic, ACER, 1967. 170p. (Monographs on
Secondary Education, no 2).
'One of the purposes ... is to give enough details of the running
of a comprehensive school to give useful suggestions to those
teachers and administrators who feel that the ideas are well worthy
of trial'.

(1527) McCULLOCH, R. W. School organisation; working papers
for the ACER research conference, May 1967. Hawthorn, Vic,
ACER, 19 67. 10 leaves.

(1528) WESTERN Australian Federation of Parents and Citizens
Associations. Organisation and administration of high school
canteens in Western Australia. Canb, Govt Pr, 1967. 55p.

1968 (1529) SEMINAR on Educational Administration, Adult Education
Centre, Wangaratta, Victoria, 1968. Educational administration,
Part 1. Basics; proceedings of a two day seminar for principals,
headmasters and headmistresses, August 1-2 1968. Wangaratta,
Vic, Adult Education Centre, 1968. 100p.

(1530) TASMANIA. Education Department. The school in society;
the report of the committee set up to investigate the role of the
school in society. Hobart, 1968. 77p.

(1531) THOMAS, K. A. Hush, the neglected minority report of the
Tasmanian State Committee on the Role of the School in Society,
July 1967-August 1968. Hobart, the Author, [1968?]. 64 leaves.

(1532) VICTORIAN Teachers Union. Administration of the primary
school. Melb, 1968. 84p.

1969 (1533) DEVIN, M. An old school meets new problems. Syd,
Govt Pr, 1969. 7p.

(1534) PETTIT, I. A. and Jansson, R. The organisation of classes
in a high school. Syd, Dept of Education Inservice Training Branch,
[1969?]. 31 leaves.

(1535) SEMINAR on Educational Administration, Adult Education
Centre, Wangaratta, Victoria, 1969. Educational administration,
Part 2. The role of the principal; proceedings of a two day
seminar for principals, and senior teachers, April 17-18 1969.
Wangaratta, Vic, 1969. 92p.

(1536) SEMINAR on Educational Administration. Adult Education
Centre, Wangaratta, Victoria, 1969. Educational administration,
[Part 3]. a. Supervision, b. Curriculum development, c. Bureau-
cracy in schools; proceedings of a two day seminar for principals
and senior teachers, October 1969. Wangaratta, Vic, Adult
Education Centre, 1969. 92p.

1970 (1537) AUSTRALIAN College of Education. Queensland Chapter.
Planning and organisation for better schools; proceedings of a
conference ... held at the Toowoomba Grammar School, 10-12
October 1969. Brisb, 1970. 59p.

(1538) SCHOENHEIMER, H. P. Good schools. Melb, National
Press, 1970. 128p.

(1539) SEMINAR on Educational Administration, Centre for
Continuing Education, Wangaratta, Victoria, 1970. Educational
administration, Part 4. Problem solving in schools; proceedings of
a two day seminar workshop for principals, and senior teachers,
April 2-3 1970. Wangaratta, Vic, Continuing Education Centre,
1970.

(1540) WALKER, W. G. Theory and practice in educational
administration. St Lucia, Qld, Univ of Qld Press, 1970. 214p.

1971 (1541) AUSTRALIAN College of Education. Queensland Chapter.
Criteria of school effectiveness; proceedings of a conference ...
October, 1970. Brisb, 1971. 41p.
Contents: Perceptions of quality education by W. Hamilton; Some
indices of an effective school by W. J. Campbell; Some implications
of the Radford Report by M. A. Howell; The evaluative process -
an interdisciplinary approach by K. Tronc.

(1542) VICTORIA. Education Department. Curriculum Standing
Committee for Technical Schools. The community school; a
proposal. [Melb, 1971]. 5 leaves.

1972 (1543) ALLOM, R. and Schultz, P. Learning place: based on
final year design thesis (1971) B. Arch, Melbourne University .
Melb, 1972. 1 vol (various pagination).

(1544) INDEX to Australian innovative schools, Armidale, 1972.
1 vol (unpaged).

(1545) VICTORIA. Education Department. Open education; its development in the primary schools of the Sunshine Inspectorate. Melb, 1972. 76p.

(ii) Private Schools

1940 (1546) AUSTRALIAN National Travel Association. Australian schools [statistical information regarding Australian boarding schools] with introduction by G. S. Browne. Melb, 1940. 21p.

1950 (1547) BEAN, C. E. W. Here, my son; an account of the independent and other corporate boys schools of Australia. Syd, A & R, 1950. 271p.

(1548) DOCKER, R. B. Harriet Christina Newcomb and Margaret Emily Hodge; values and basis of their work in education. Syd, Newcomb-Hodge Fellowship, 1950. 10p.

1953 (1549) RADFORD, W. C. The non-government schools of Australia; a descriptive and statistical account. Melb, MUP for the ACER, 1953. 133p. (ACER Research Series, no 66).

1962 (1550) CARROLL, J. Independent schools in a free society; the contemporary pattern of education in Australia. Syd, Catholic Press Newspaper Co, 1962. 20p.

1965 (1551) CATHOLIC Education Advisory Council. What we are doing for Catholic schools in the Archdiocese of Melbourne. Melb, 1965. 12p.

(1552) HAWKINS, T. M. The Queensland great public schools; a history. Brisb, Jacaranda Press, 1965. 335p.

1967 (1553) McKEOWN, P. J. and Hone, B. W. , editors. The independent school, papers presented to the Headmasters Conference. Melb, OUP, 1967. 189p.
Papers selected from those presented to the Headmasters Conference of the Independent Schools of Australia, 1931-66.

1969 (1554) THE Australians' guide to Australia's top private schools and colleges. Syd, 1969. 1 vol (unpaged). 2nd edition 1970.

(1555) BOURKE, J. E. Australian Catholic schools into the seventies. Hawthorn, Vic, ACER, 1969. 43p. (Quarterly Review of Australian Education, vol 3, no 2).

1970 (1556) WESTERN Australia. Education Department. Report on the needs of Catholic schools in Western Australia, 1970-74. Perth, Govt Pr, 1970. 144p.

1972 (1557) ARCHDALE, H. E. Indiscretions of a headmistress. Syd, A & R, 1972. 226p.

(iii) Histories of State Schools

1922 (1558) HOCKING, J. The story of Melbourne High School, 1905-21.
Melb, Speciality Press, 1922. 80p.

1946 (1559) MARTINDALE, H. G. The story of the Shepparton High
School. Shepparton, Vic, School Advisory Council, 1946. 79p.

1947 (1560) EWERS, J. K. Perth Boys' School, 1847-1947; the story
of the first hundred years of a great school with a background of
the history of education in Western Australia. Perth, the School,
1947. 183p.

1948 (1561) MASLIN, J. S. Hagley; the story of a Tasmanian area school.
Melb, Georgian House, 1948. 98p.

1956 (1562) HOOPER, A. The story of Flinders School, Geelong, 1856-1956
Geelong, Vic, Mercer Print, 1956. 52p.
About Matthew Flinders Girls Secondary School, Geelong, Vic.

1957 (1563) MADDERN, I. T. 100 Years history of Wodonga State School,
no 37, 1857-1957. Wodonga, Vic, the School Committee, 1957.
16p.

1959 (1564) BAYLEY, W. A. Ninety years on; celebrating the ninetieth
anniversay of the opening on 7 July 1869 of Bulli Public School, 1869-
1959. Kiama, NSW, the Author, 1959. 26p.

1961 (1565) 'FOOTSCRAY Advertiser'. Geelong Road State Schoo, no 253;
centenary, 1861-1961. Melb, 1961. 24p.

(1566) HOY, A. A city built to music; the history of University
High School, Melbourne, 1910-60. Melb, Univ High School, 1961.
178p.

(1567) KIAMA Primary School, NSW. Kiama Primary School
Centenary, 1861-1961. 1961. 55p.

(1568) NEW South Wales. Department of Education Division of
Research and Planning. Ulladulla Public School Centenary, 1861-
1961; an historical account. Ulladulla, 1961. 16p.

(1569) STOCKTON Public School Centenary Committee. Stockton
Public School centenary, 1861-1961. Stockton, NSW, 1961. 16p.

1962 (1570) STOREY, H. M. History of North Sydney High School,
1912-62. Syd, Old Falconians Union, 1962. 71p.

1963 (1571) PUGH, A. V., compiler. History of the Murray Bridge High
School, 1913-63. Murray Bridge, SA, the School, 1963. 12p.

1965 (1572) ARARAT, Victoria, State School. Centenary, Ararat State
School no 800; souvenir booklet. 1965. 20p.

(1573) THE FIRST three years in the life of the Campbell Primary
School. Canb, 1965. 6p.

(1574) JERVIS, J. Canterbury Boys High School [NSW] ; a history,
1918-50. Syd, Old Cantabrians Union, 1965. 32p.

(1575) MACFARLANE, C. W. Burnie High School golden jubilee, 1916-65. Burnie, Tas, the School, 1965. 59p.

1966 (1576) BRAGGETT, E. J. From convict era to modern times; Newcastle East School, 1816-1966. Newcastle, NSW, Newcastle East Public School Parents and Citizens Assn, 1966. 96p.

(1577) MADDERN, I. T. , editor. History of Morwell High School, 1956. Morwell, Vic, the School, 1966-70. 5 vols.

(1578) NAIRNS, M. G. , compiler. The history of Russell Vale Public School, 1954-65. Russell Vale, NSW, the School, 1966. 17p.

1967 (1579) COOERWULL Public School, Lithgow, NSW. Cooerwull Public School centenary, 1867-1967; souvenir booklet. Lithgow, NSW, 1967. 35p.

(1580) LOCKTON, H. and I. Centenary, Wardell School and district, 1867-1967. Wardell, NSW, the Authors, 1967. 64p.

(1581) MADDERN, I. T. The history of Toongabbie, Victoria, 1862-1967. Toongabbie, Vic, School Centenary Celebrations Committee, 1967. 20p.

(1582) MILTHORPE Public School, NSW. Milthorpe Public School, 1867-1967. 1967. 26p.

(1583) WARREN Central School, NSW. Warren Central School, 1867-1967, centenary history; one hundred years of education. 1967. 27p.

1968 (1584) APPIN, NSW, Public School. Appin Public School Centenary, 1868-1968. 1968. 11p.

(1585) BAULKHAM HILLS. Public School, NSW, Souvenir magazine; centenary of education, 1868-1968, 1968. 48p.

(1586) BULAHDELAH Central School, NSW. Bulahdelah Central School centenary, 1868-1968. Taree, NSW, 1968. 55p.

(1587) BUNGENDORE Public School, NSW. Centenary of education in Bungendore 1868-1968. 1968. 20p.

(1588) CHATSWORTH Island, NSW. Public School. Centenary of education, Chatsworth ... 1868-1968. 1968. 52p.

(1589) CORAKI, NSW. Central School. Coraki Central School; 100 years 1868-1968. 1968. 60p.

(1590) KANGALOON East Public School, NSW. A history of education in East Kangaloon. 1968. 19p.

(1591) MILLICENT, SA. Primary School. Back to school at Millicent. 1968. 12p.
'This booklet has been produced to commemorate the 94 years of service to the community of the Millicent Primary School'.

(1592) MITCHELL, K. B. , editor. A history of Dandenong High School, 1919-68. Dandenong, Vic, Dandenong High School Advisory Council, 1968. 64p.

(1593) NARRABRI, NSW. Centenary of education 1868-1968. Narrabri Primary School and Narrabri High School, 1968. 56p.

(1594) PARKES Public School, NSW. A century of public education in Parkes; history of Parkes (Currajong) Public School, established in August 1868. 1968. 1 vol (unpaged).

(1595) PETERS, M. The story of a school; a centenary of public education in Bankstown 1868-1968. Bankstown, NSW, Bankstown North Public School, 1968. 15p.

(1596) REGENTVILLE Public School, NSW. Centenary 1868-1968. 1968. 15p.

(1597) RYDE Public School, NSW. Ryde Public School centenary book, 1868-1968. 1968. 24p.

(1598) WIANGAREE Public School, NSW. Diamond jubilee, 1908-68. 1968. 8p.

1969 (1599) CROSS, M. E. , compiler. Eight Mile Plains State School (school no 34); centenary booklet, June 1869 to June 1969. Eight Mile Plains, Qld, Parents & Citizens Assn, 1969. 16p.

(1600) EKERT, A. E. Pyramul Public School centenary, 1869-1969. Pyramul, NSW, 1969. 16p.

(1601) ELDEN, J. C. , editor. Who's who of notable old boys. 2nd ed. Carlton, Vic, Melbourne High School Old Boys Assn, 1969. 19p. Bound with MHS Register & Old Boys Directory 1905-27, entry 1614.

(1602) GARDNER, J. C. , compiler. A history of Kerang High School, 1919-69. Kerang, Vic, the Compiler, 1969. 86p.

(1603) GREEN, L. L. , editor. Koala; Tamworth High School, 1919-69. Tamworth, NSW, the School, 1969. 151p.

(1604) JERILDERIE Public School, NSW. Jerilderie, 1869-1969. 1969. 13 leaves.

(1605) McLEOD, K. P. State School no 3941, Coburg West; an historical survey. Coburg West Primary School, Vic 1969. 10 leaves.

(1606) MILLS, A. , compiler. Schools of the Berriwillock district, Victoria. Berriwillock Historical Society, 1969. 1 vol (unpaged).

(1607) MULCAHY, D. and Lee, C. N. A history of education; Kangaloon Public School Centenary, 1869-1969. Kangaloo., NSW, 1969. 15p.

(1608) MURRAY, K. A history of the Ballarat Technical School, Victoria. The School, 1969. 67p.

(1609) SPRING Terrace Public School, NSW. Celebrating the centenary of education in the Spring Terrace district. Orange, NSW, 1969. 11p.

(1610) SULLIVAN, J. J. , editor. A century of education, 1869-1969. Kialla, NSW, Kialla Public School, 1969. 52p.

1970 (1611) BARRIE, E. and Rogers, M. The first one hundred years, 1870-1970; Melton State School no 430. Melton, Vic, the School, 1970. 27p.

(1612) BOWERS, D. H. , editor. The Ballarat School of Mines; retrospect 1870-1970. Ballarat, Vic, School of Mines and Industries, 1970. 40p.

(1613) COONABARABRAN Public School, NSW. Coonabarabran Public School centenary, 1870-1970. 1970. 40p.

(1614) ELDEN, J. C. , editor. The Melbourne High School register and old boys directory 1905-1927. Carlton, Vic, Melbourne High School Old Boys' Association, 1970. 92p.
Bound with the editors' Who's who of notable old boys as vol 20, no 9 (no 139) of The Old Unicornian. See also entry 1601, page 134.

(1615) FORD, J. , editor. Hunter's Hill Primary School Centenary, 1870-1970. Hunter's Hill Primary School P & C Assn, NSW, 1970. 16p.

(1616) JAMES, J. R. and G. Kincumber Public School centenary, 1870-1970. Kincumber, NSW, the Authors, 1970. 24p.

(1617) LYNCH, J. M. Centenary 1870-1970; Merimbula Public School. Merimbula, NSW, 1970. 24 leaves.

(1618) NICHOLLS, R. A. A history of Highton and its school. Highton, Vic, Highton School Committee, 1970. 38p.

(1619) POTTER, J. L. , editor. Salisbury Public School, 1877-1970. Salisbury, SA, the School, 1970. 32p.

(1620) SPENCER, R. F. Hill End Public School Centenary, 1870-1970. Hill End, NSW, 1970. 16p.

1971 (1621) BARKER, A. O. A brief history of Forth State School. Forth, Tas, 1971. 8p.

(1622) DELEGATE Public School, 1827-1971, and a short history of Delegate. Delegate, NSW. 1971. 24p.

(1623) GEHAM State School centenary, 1871-1971; souvenir brochure. Geham, Qld, 1971. 36p.

(1624) KANGAROO Valley Public School; 100 years of education, 1871-1971. Kangaroo Valley, NSW, School Centenary Celebrations Committee, 1971. 32p.

(1625) KERKHAM, A. E. Lilydale School centenary. Lilydale, Tas, Parents & Friends Assn, 1971. 12p.

(1626) LEWIS, B. G. , editor. Blacktown Public School centenary, 1871-1971. Blacktown, NSW, 1971. 43p.

(1627) MULLENGANDRA School Centenary 1871-1971. Mullengandra, NSW, 1971. 36p.

(1628) NEW South Wales. Department of Education. Division
of Research and Planning. Drummoyne Public Schoo, 1886-1971.
Syd, 1971. 12p.

(1629) NEW Wouth Wales. Department of Education. Division of
Research and Planning. The history of Grose Vale Public School,
1871-1971. Grose Vale Public School Centenary Committee, 1971.
26p.

(1630) SULLIVAN, J. Peakhurst Public School centenary, 1871-1971.
Peakhurst, NSW, P & C Assn, 1971. 28p.

1972 (1631) BREMNER, G. A. Onward and upward Kyneton High School
diamond jubilee, 1912-72. Kyneton Guardian, Vic, 1972. 107p.

(1632) FORSTER Central School, 1872-1972. Forster, NSW,
Central School Centenary Committee, 1972. 39p.

(1633) MACQUEEN, E. M. , editor. 1141 Bruthen, the first hundred
years. Bruthen, Vic, the Editor, 1972. 20p.

(1634) ROBERTSON P & C Association. Centenary of education,
1872-1972. Robertson, NSW, 1972. 36p.

(iv) Histories of Private Schools

1914 (1635) WILMOT, R. W. E. , editor. Liber Melburniensis, 1858-
1914; a history of the Church of England Grammar School, Melbourne.
Melb, Arbuckle, Waddell & Fawkner, 1914. 468p.

1926 (1636) FRIENDS High School, Hobart, Tas. Scheme for alterations
and additions to the school buildings. Hobart, 1926. 1 vol (unpaged).

(1637) SCOTCH College, Melbourne. History of Scotch College,
Melbourne, 1851-1925. Melb, 1926. 674p.

1935 (1638) RAIT, B. W. The official history of the Hutchins School.
Hobart, Walch, 1935. 152p.

1936 (1639) METHODIST Ladies College, Burwood, NSW. Jubilee
souvenir, 1886-1936. Syd, 1936. 174p.

(1640) STEEL, W. A. and Sloman, C. W. The history of All Saints
College, Bathurst, 1873-1934. Syd, A & R, 1936. 227p.
Second edition by W. A. Steel and J. M. Antill brings the history
up to 1951 (published in 1952).

1938 (1641) MELBOURNE Church of England Grammar School. Grimwade
House, Melbourne Church of England Grammar School; years 1918-38.
Melb, 1938. 72p.

1939 (1642) BURTON, A. Hale School, Perth; the story of its foundation
and early years, 1858-1900. Perth, 1939. 50p.

1940 (1643) GRAHAM, J. A. The Creswick Grammar School history. Melb, Brown, Prior, Anderson, 1940. 169p.

1941 (1644) WESLEY College, Melbourne. The history of Wesley College, 1920-40. Melb, McCarron, Bird, 1941. 144p.

1944 (1645) HALL, J. T. History of St Stanislaus College, Bathurst. Bathurst, NSW, the College, 1944. 225p.

(1646) KING'S College, Adelaide, SA. The friendly years; King's College 1924-44. Adel, the College, 1944. 72p.

1945 (1647) ROWLAND, E. C. Story of Cranbrook. Syd, D. S. Ford, 1945. 31p.

1946 (1648) GEORGE, E. The Wilderness book. Adel, Hassell Press, 1946. 40p.
History of the Wilderness School Ltd, Menindie, SA.

(1649) HUTCHINS School Centenary Magazine, 1846-1946. Hobart, the School, 1946. 136p.

(1650) RAIT, B. W. The story of the Launceston Church Grammar School. Launceston, the School Centenary Committee, 1946. 202p.

1947 (1651) PRICE, A. G. The Collegiate School of St Peter, 1847-1947; being an illustrated record of the first hundred years. Adel, Council of Governors, 1947. 77p.

1948 (1652) CANBERRA. Church of England Girls Grammar School. Coming-of-age celebrations, 1927-48. Canb, Board of Directors, 1948. 7p.

(1653) MORRIS, W. P. F. Sons of Magnus; first steps of a Queensland school. Brisb, Brooks, 1948. 150p.
About Brisbane Church of England Grammar School.

(1654) WOODLANDS Church of England Girls Grammar School, Glenelg, SA. Woodlands; the first twenty-five years, 1923-48. Glenelg, SA, 1948. 110p.

1949 (1655) FREEMAN, G. P. History of Somerville House, the Brisbane High School for Girls, 1899-1949. Brisb, Smith & Paterson, 1949. 100p.

(1656) MELLER, M. The Stanley Grammar School, Watervale, and Joseph Stear Carlyon Cole. Adel, Pioneers Assn of SA, 1949. 14p.

1950 (1657) WALTON, G. M. The building of a tradition, 1908-45. Perth, Imperial Printing Co, 1950. 113p.
About Methodist Ladies College, WA.

1951 (1658) GIRTON House Girls Grammar School, Adelaide. Old Scholars Book Committee. The Girton book, anniversary and memorial year 1951. Adel, 1951. 66p.

(1659) HOLME, E. R. Shore; the Sydney Church of England Grammar School. Syd, A & R, 1951. 167p.

(1660) WARD, J. F. Prince Alfred College; the story of the first eighty years, 1867-1948. Adel, Gillingham, 1951. 256p.

1952 (1661) FLOWER, M. The story of Ascham school. Syd, Council of Governors of Ascham school, 1952. 47p.

(1662) NICHOLSON, G. H. , editor. First hundred years; Scotch College, Melbourne, 1851-1951. Melb, Old Scotch Collegians Assn, 1952. 743p.

1956 (1663) PRESBYTERIAN Ladies College, Pymble, NSW. Presbyterian Ladies College Pymble, 1916-56. Syd, 1956. 64p.

(1664) SOUTHALL, I. The story of the Hermitage; the first fifty years of the Geelong Church of England Girls Grammar School. Melb, Cheshire, 1956. 94p.

1957 (1665) DANIELL, H. Y. History of Ruyton, 1878-1956. Melb, Ramsay Ware, 1957. 144p.
Ruyton Girls Grammar School, Melbourne.

(1666) METHODIST Ladies College, Hawthorn, Vic. Seventy-five years at Methodist Ladies College, Hawthorn, 1882-1957. Melb, Spectator Pub Co, 1957. 127p.

(1667) THE SYDNEIAN. Sydney Grammar School; the centenary, 1957. Syd, Trustees of Syd Grammar School, 1957. 155p.
Centenary number of 'The Sydneian'.

1958 (1668) ROSALIE, Sister. Perth College, 1902-52. Perth, Univ of WA Press, 1958. 62p.

(1669) SYDNEY. Church of England Girls Grammar School Council. Sydney Church of England Girls Grammar School, 1895-1955. Syd 1958. 255p.

1960 (1670) REID, M. O. The ladies came to stay; a study of the education of girls at the Presbyterian Ladies College, Melbourne, 1875-1960. Melb, Council of the Presbyterian Ladies College, 1960. 312p.

1961 (1671) MUNRO, M. The old Aspinall's day; the Scots College, Sydney from 1893-1913, including a chronological table to 1958. Syd, Wentworth Press, 1961. 143p.

(1672) NOTMAN, G. C. and Keith, B. R. The Geelong College, 1861-1961. Geelong, The College Council and the Old Geelong Collegian's Assn, 1961. 240p.

(1673) OATS, W. N. The Friends School, 1887-1961; the seventy-fifth anniversary. Hobart, the School, 1961. 127p.

1962 (1674) AIKMAN, R. G. and Honniball, J. H. M. The Chapel of Saints Mary-and George, Guildford Grammar School; a history. Guildford, WA, Council of Guildford Grammar School, 1962. 121p.

(1675) ANGOVE, D. C. A tribute to Caroline Jacob from the Tormore Old Scholars Association. Adel, the Assn, 1962. 15p. '... the most eminent pioneer of modern ideas for the education of women in South Australia'.

1963 (1676) ALLSOPP, J. H. A century history of the Ipswich Grammar School, 1863-1963. Ipswich, Qld, Grammar School, 1963. 139p.

(1677) MACMILLAN, D. S. Newington College, 1863-1963. Syd, the College, 1963. 184p.

(1678) TUCKEY, E. Fifty years at Frensham; a history of an Australian school. Mittagong, NSW, Winifred West Schools, 1963. 160p.

1964 (1679) MEIN, W. G. History of Ballarat College, 1864-1964. Ballarat, Vic, Ballarat College Council, 1964. 215p.

1965 (1680) HARPER, J. B. What matter I; the founding of a school. Ivanhoe, Vic, Ivanhoe Grammar School, 1965. 144p.

(1681) MELBOURNE Church of England Grammar School. Liber Melburniensis; centenary edition. 4th ed. Melb, 1965. 614p.

(1682) TAYLOR, F. Schooldays with the Simpsons, 1899-1906; the early history of Mentone Girls Grammar School, Victoria. Tirau, NZ, S. G. Barnett, [1965?] . 64p.

1966 (1683) HAY, O. J. and Reid, M. O. The chronicles of Clyde. Melb, Brown, Prior, Anderson, 1966. 261p. About Clyde School for Girls, Woodend, Vic.

(1684) MUNRO, M. Shirley, the story of a school in Sydney, compiled for the Shirley Old Girls Union by May Munro. Killara, the Union, 1966. 128p. History of Shirley School, Edgecliffe, NSW.

1967 (1685) BLAINEY, G. , Morrissey, J. and Hulme, S. E. K. Wesley College, the first hundred years. Melb, Wesley College in association with R & M, 1967. 240p.

(1686) MONTGOMERY, E. H. and Darling, J. R. Timbertop; an innovation in Australian education. Melb, Cheshire, 1967. 167p. Timbertop is an annexe to Geelong Grammar and is situated at Mansfield, Vic.

(1687) ST STANISLAUS College, Bathurst, NSW. St Stanislaus College, 1867-1967; centenary reflections. Bathurst, NSW, 1967. 57p.

(1688) SCHUBERT, J. A. A history of Warracknabeal College, 1901-12. Warracknabeal, Vic, the Author, 1967. 15p. The College closed in 1912.

1968 (1689) BURROWS, D. History of Abbotsleigh, Wahroonga, NSW. Council of Abbotsleigh. 1968. 124p.

(1690) CHILD, A. C. Cranbrook; the first fifty years, 1918-68.
Syd, Cranbrook School, 1968. 278p.

(1691) WILLEY, K. The first hundred years; the story of Brisbane
Grammar School, 1868-1968. Melb, Brisbane Grammar School and
Macmillan, 1968. 385p.

1969 (1692) COWPERTHWAITE, D. Morongo; a history of the Presbyterian Girls College, Geelong, Victoria, Australia, 1920-70.
Melb, Lothian, 1969. 113p.

(1693) JONES, J. and Morrison, M. Walford, a history of the
school; a memorial to Mabel Jewell Baker. Hyde Park, SA,
Walford Old Scholars Assn, 1969. 111p.

1970 (1694) BROWN, P. L. Geelong Grammar School; the first
historical phase. Geelong, Vic, Geelong Historical Society,
1970. 31p.

(1695) RILETT, W., compiler. Immanuel College, Novar Gardens;
a history of the years 1945-70. Novar Gardens, SA, Immanuel
College 75th Anniversary Committee, 1970. 40p.

1971 (1696) CLARKE, J. and Cochran, M. The lamp burns brightly;
the first century of Clarendon College, Ballarat, 1868-1968.
Ballarat, Vic, the College, 1971. 120p.

(1697) HANSEN, I. V. Nor free nor secular; six independent
schools in Victoria. A first sample. Melb, 1971. 323p.
Surveys Geelong College, Geelong Church of England Grammar
School, Melbourne Church of England Grammar School, Scotch
College, Wesley College, Xavier College.

(1698) JUDD, T. Fifty years will be long enough; a school
porter's story. Melb, National Press, 1971. 208p.

(1699) SPEEDY, C. L., editor. From these things unto greater;
a history of Oakburn College, Methodist Ladies College, Launceston.
Launceston, Tas, the College, 1971. 79p.

(1700) TUCKER, L. Splendoured road from Dorset; a centenary
history of Penleigh Presbyterian Ladies College. Moonee Ponds,
Vic, the College, 1971. 115p.

(1701) WOLLACOTT, E. H. Westminster School [SA]: the first
decade, 1961-71. Netley, SA, 1971. 103p.

1972 (1702) MILNE, B. W. and McKellar, D. W. Cromarty School for
Girls, Melbourne, 1897-1923. Melbourne, Stockland Press, 1972.
83p.

Name Index

Includes names of people, institutions, organizations, societies, conferences, seminars, etc.

Subject Index

Sources Consulted

Annual catalogue of Australian publications. Canb, National Library of Australia, 1936-60.

Australian national bibliography. Canb, National Library of Australia, 1961-72.

Ferguson, J.A. Bibliography of Australia, 1851-1900. Syd, A & R, 1941-69.

Foxcroft, B. The Australian catalogue; a reference index to the books and periodicals published and still current in the Commonwealth of Australia. Lond, H. Pordes, 1961. (Reprint of 1911 edition).

Lewin, P.E., compiler. Best books on Australia and New Zealand; an annotated bibliography. Lond, Royal Empire Society, 1946.

McGrath, W.A. New Guineana, or books of New Guinea 1942-65; a bibliography of books printed between 1942 and 1964. Port Moresby, the Compiler, 1965.

Mitchell Library, Sydney. Dictionary catalog of printed books. Boston, Mass, G. K. Hall, 1968.

Royal Commonwealth Society, London. Library. Subject catalogue of the library. 1931. (vol 2 Commonwealth of Australia).

Spence, S.A., compiler. A bibliography of selected books and pamphlets relating to Australia, 1610-1880. Mitcham, England, 1952.

Contractions Used in Imprints

Adel	Adelaide		Research in England and
A & R	Angus & Robertson		Wales
Assn	Association	no	Number
A'sian	Australasian	NSW	New South Wales
ANZAAS	Australian and New Zealand Association for the Advancement of Science	NUAUS	National Union of Australian University Students
		NY	New York
		NZ	New Zealand
ACE	Australian College of Education	OUP	Oxford University Press
		p	page(s)
ACER	Australian Council for Educational Research	PNG	Papua New Guinea
		pseud	pseudonym
ANU	Australian National University	pub	publisher, published
		Qld	Queensland
AUS	Australian Union of Students	R & M	Robertson & Mullen
		SA	South Australia
Brisb	Brisbane	SAIT	South Australian Institute of Teachers
bros	Brothers		
Canb	Canberra	Syd	Sydney
co	Company	Tas	Tasmania
Dept	Department	TPNG	Territory of Papua New Guinea
Edinb	Edinburgh		
Govt	Government	Vic	Victoria
Inst	Institute	VICSSO	Victorian Council of State School Organizations
Lond	London		
Melb	Melbourne	VIER	Victorian Institute of Educational Research
MUP	Melbourne University Press		
		vol(s)	volume(s)
NEF	New Education Fellowship	WA	Western Australia
		WEA	Workers Educational Association
NFER	National Foundation for Educational	Well	Wellington, New Zealand